Football's Multiple
Slot-T Attack

Football's Multiple Slot-T Attack

Jim R. McClain

Parker Publishing Co., Inc.

West Nyack,
New York

Library of Congress Cataloging in Publication Data

McClain, Jim R
    Football's multiple slot-T attack.

    1. Football--Offense. I. Title.
GV951.8.M32   796.33'22   73-16361
ISBN 0-13-324129-7

Kick Off

(The Multiple Slot-T offense provides the two central qualities a good offense must have: It provides the ground game/passing game ratio to any degree the coach wishes to use it. It also provides through series action a great deal of easily attainable deception, especially vital when a team meets an opponent that is physically superior.)

Though most coaches advocate strong defensive play, the "How?" many of them ask first is "How do we score?" The expression, "If you prevent your opponent from scoring, the worst you can do is tie," isn't applicable to an entire season. Many strong defensive teams have become complacent and then vulnerable because their offense couldn't score.

With this "How to score?" in mind, the Multiple Slot-T Offense was put together. It represents the best techniques that have been proven to generate a scoring punch. It is an offense that has averaged 24 points per game over a consecutive six-year period, with a 30 point average per game during one of those years. The same offense with few adjustments has been used for a passing team or a running team, depending on the personnel available.

(Any offense must have a strong off-tackle series, the primary idea of the Multiple Slot-T. The offense attempts to penetrate the off-tackle area by using a few techniques that place considerable mental pressure on the defensive tackles, ends, corners, or halfbacks, depending on the alignment of the defense.)

Some of the attack is a head-up one-on-one situation which the very nature of the game provides, but most of the running game employs techniques other than power. The running game toward the tight end side is aimed at the defensive tackle. By employing the option block by the strong-side tackle, it is possible to run the inside or outside belly at that tackle. The threat of the double team by the tackle and slotback or tight end further complicates the play of the defensive tackle, and allows the offensive tackle to conquer the defensive tackle.

The attack away from the formation is designed to place the pressure primarily on the defensive end. The threat of the sweep, option, quick-pitch, reverse, and sprint toward the defensive end, along with the possible double-coverage on the split end, enables the offense to have a highly potent off-side attack.

Oddly enough, with emphasis upon getting outside, one of the best ground gainers the offense has is the inside trap. Perhaps it isn't so odd after all if we have convinced the defense we are coming outside, thus providing the opportunity to counter to the inside.

⌊ The Multiple Slot-T is structured to attack each area with at least two of the best techniques possible. By employing a shift to the various formations and using motion prior to the snap, the defense will be forced to make several adjustments which will result in defensive breakdowns. This will also prevent the defense from being in an attacking position and probably reduce their aggressiveness.⌉

The Multiple Slot-T Attack is easily adjusted to be a ground–oriented or a pass-oriented offense. I was fortunate to have an exceptional passer in Chip Howard, who was an All-American quarterback. In three seasons Chip passed for 47 touchdowns and ran for 27 more while compiling 5,100 yards in total offense. The Multiple Slot-T Offense was flexible enough to utilize the talent of this exceptional quarterback.

⌈ Probably one of the greatest features of the Multiple Slot-T is the ease with which the system can be taught. It is organized and uses simple terminology—two things which are very important in teaching any system. If an athlete has few problems in learning the responsibilities of his position, he can get on with the task of mastering the required techniques.⌉

Part II of the book deals with the running game. In these chapters the blocking rules for the hole or opening will be given first. The play will then be diagrammed against several favorite defensive alignments (such as the Okla. 5-2, 4-3, Split-6 or 4-4, 5-3, and Wide 6-2). This will show how the blocking rules apply. In Part III of the book we will see how to establish pass routes without having to memorize countless patterns.

t This book offers an offensive system that has been tried and proved. It is flexible enough to vary the attack in any manner the coach chooses. The ease with which it can be learned provides the athlete with increased confidence. The Multiple Slot-T Attack is fundamental and at the same time explosive. 7

Jim McClain

Contents

PART III: MULTIPLE SLOT-T PASSING GAME

The pass zones: terminology of pass zones • advantages of pass zones • required adjustments • coaching points for an effective passing attack: the passer • the receiver • the coach

The sprint pass protection • the play action protection • pocket protection • the moving pocket protection • the quick-pass protection • the advantages and disadvantages of each type of protection

The out routes • the take-off routes • the flag, streak, and hook routes • the post and trail-in routes • the wide delay and look-in routes • the underneath post pattern • the tailback and the fullback pass routes • the screen passes • the draw • special passes

PART IV: MULTIPLE SLOT-T GAME MECHANICS

Discovering opponent's weaknesses: defensive personnel • alignment weaknesses of the defense • defensive techniques and

Chapter 10—Preparing the Multiple Slot-T Game Plan *(continued)*

*coverages • defensive adjustments • utilizing the scouting report •
the responsibility of coaches during the game • the halftime •
mental factors • game plan organization—coaches' meetings*

*The shift • the use of motion • audibles • starting the back in
motion • signal calling • reading the defense: attacking the 5-4
defense • attacking the 5-3 defense • attacking the split-4 defense •
passing against a three-deep zone secondary • attacking a four-deep
zone • defeating a man-to-man coverage • the two-minute offense*

Football's Multiple Slot-T Attack

PART 1

Chapter 1

Selecting Personnel for the Multiple Slot-T Attack

A complete evaluation of each member of the squad, by the coaching staff, is vital when selecting the personnel for the various positions of the offensive team. Each position has to be carefully analyzed in relation to the degree of importance placed on that position in the overall offensive scheme. Questions have to be asked in relation to, "What do we expect that position to do? Are we asking too much? Can that position be filled with the personnel we have?" The overall strength of the offense can be determined, to some degree, by answering these questions.

INTERIOR LINEMEN

The Tackles

The strength of an offensive team that runs the football considerably is measured by the overall ability of the tackles. Here is where the running game will succeed or fail. The primary objective of any offense is to run off-tackle where a small number of defensive personnel are protecting a sizable area of the football field. An offensive tackle who can control his area is a tremendous asset to the offense. The Multiple Slot-T places a high premium on the tackles. Since the tendency of most teams is to be right-handed (run to the right a higher percentage of the time), the best offensive tackle should be the right tackle. This will make him the strong-side tackle when the offense is in right formation. The strong-side tackle will usually have a head-up or one-on-one situation with a defensive tackle while the weak-side tackle, because of the split-end alignment to his side, often has an eagle or a similar alignment which places a tackle in the gap between him and the guard. A cut-off or seal block is easier to accomplish than a drive block.

The Guards

The guard who has the greater ability to pull and trap should be the left guard. Even if there is no tendency to run to the right or to the left, pulling to the right is the easier maneuver for most high school linemen. If you prefer to use the same guard when trapping or pulling to lead block, it will probably go unnoticed. If it is detected you will know it soon enough.

The Center

The fifth best lineman in the Multiple Slot-T offense is the center. The exchange of the football between the center and the quarterback is the most important event on the field at the time of the snap, but otherwise the center is not that vital. On the trap plays he either has help from the guard or has an angle. No center can use a cut-off block on a quick middle guard who is reading the initial action of the quarterback. Of course the center should not be led to believe he is insignificant. If the center hustles he might be able to make contact with the middle guard, who is waiting to make the tackle on the ball carrier.

The Ends

Usually when the offensive formation is to the right side, the left end is the split end while the right end plays a tight end position. This varies slightly depending on the formation used. The opposite of this is true for the tight end position as far as personnel is concerned. The reason for this will be explained in detail in a later chapter, but perhaps it would be wise to give the most important reason now. To gain part of the multiple factor in the Multiple Slot-T Attack a shift from a Power I formation into one of four other formations is used. To keep the eventual formation concealed from the defense it is necessary to have some versatility among the ends. There are many ways of employing the shift, but this is one of the simpler ways. The best pass receiver among the ends should be the left end because he will be split more often than the right end. The blocking ability of the ends should be strongly emphasized.

THE BACKS

Fullback

Ruggedness is definitely a key factor when selecting the fullback. The fullback is largely responsible for the success of the Multiple Slot-T. The ability to get necessary yardage, aggressiveness when blocking an opponent, and durability are necessary trademarks of the fullback.

The Tailback and Slotback

The tailback and the slotback will be discussed at the same time, since each halfback will play either position depending on whether right or left formation is used. For example, when in right formation the right halfback becomes the slotback and the left halfback is the tailback. There are several reasons for having a different tailback and slotback in right and left formations. For example, an ideal slotback should possess the following abilities:

(1) Be able to double-team block with the tackle or end.
(2) Be able to effectively block a linebacker, inverted safety, etc.
(3) Possess the speed to run the outside reverse and be a deep threat in passing situations.
(4) Be a good pass Receiver.
(5) Have the acceleration to run the inside and outside traps.

A back who possesses all of these traits is rare. The tailback qualities are balance, agility, quickness to the running lane, good blocker, and an adequate pass receiver.

By combining the tailback and the slotback positions the talents of each athlete are combined, and by deploying the different formations right and left the desired match-ups to meet a given situation can be easily attained. Another advantage of this set-up is that the work load of the tailback can be shared by two ball carriers. Still another advantage—flip-flopping the backs (the same tailback and slotback all the time) and not the linemen would confuse the numerical system of the offense. If the linemen were flip-flopped the defense could key from this to determine the side of formation, thus making the shift ineffective.

The back with the greater speed should be the left halfback. He will be the tailback when right formation is used. The option, as far as the pitch is concerned, is easier to execute when moving to the right, therefore utilizing the speed of the left halfback more effectively.

The Quarterback

The Multiple Slot-T is not an offense that is built around the quarterback. The quarterback with average speed and an average passing arm can effectively operate the offense. However, the flexibility of the offense provides the opportunity to take full advantage of the abilities of the exceptional quarterback. Ball handling, footwork, faking, and executing the various pitches are essentials the quarterback develops through many hours of hard work. The quarterback will spend more time at work than any other member of the offense.

The Key Positions

The best offensive lineman is the right tackle. The left guard is the better pulling guard. The left end is the best pass receiver. The short slot, the wide slot, and the flanker are deployed right or left to take advantage of the ability of the player in that position.

Chapter 2

Developing Multiple Slot-T Formations and Alignments

The Splits of Interior Linemen

The splits of the interior linemen vary slightly from a minimum to a maximum distance. The speed of the backs, the ability and quickness of the linemen, a penetrating gap defense, the down and distance, and the position on the field are factors that determine which splits are used. Figure 2.1 shows the minimum and maximum splits taken by the interior linemen.

(LT) 24"-36" (LG) 18"-24" (C) 18"-24" (RG) 24"-36" (RT)

**Figure 2.1 Minimum-Maximum
Splits of Interior Linemen**

When running the football inside the tackles a maximum split is used, except when in a goal-line situation. A minimum split is desired when running the football off-tackle and wide. The minimum splits are also used when throwing the football. In pocket or cup protection, the minimum splits will result in less space for the defense to rush the passer by going around the offensive linemen. When employing an aggressive block for the pass there is a greater chance for solid contact with the opponent if the minimum split is used.

FORMATIONS AND ALIGNMENTS

The Multiple Slot-T Offense includes ten formations, five to the right and five to the left. The various formations indicate the positions and alignments of the back and ends.

The back who is wider than the regular alignment of a halfback or, if not wider, is the only back in a normal halfback alignment, is the format for identifying right and left formation. A normal halfback alignment would place the back behind his offensive tackle some three and one-half yards from the line of scrimmage.

**Figure 2.2 Back Wider than
Normal-Right Formation**

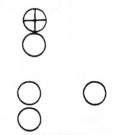

**Figure 2.3 Only Back in Normal
Alignment-Right Formation**

The Short-Slot Formations

The basic formation of the Multiple Slot-T is the short-slot and is called Right 100 and Left 100. The 100 formations represents the power attack of the offense, especially to the side of the formation.

The Alignment of the Ends in 100 Formation

The end away from the formation (in Figure 2.4 the left end and in Figure 2.5 the right end) has a minimum split of five yards and a maximum of seven. He should have a minimum split when his blocking assignment is to crack or seal. He should also have a minimum split some of the time when his split is incidental, to prevent the defense from developing keys. The end on the side of the formation, who is the tight end, is split two and one-half yards from his offensive tackle.

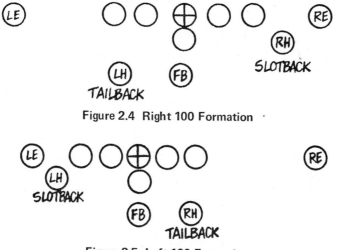

Figure 2.4 Right 100 Formation

Figure 2.5 Left 100 Formation

The Alignment of the Backs in the 100 Formation

The slotback must be at least one full yard from the line of scrimmage. His alignment splits the difference between the tackle and the end. When the slotback assumes a three point stance he should be able to touch the outside hip of the tackle with his hand if his arm is fully extended.

The alignment of the fullback never changes in any of the formations used in the Multiple Slot-T Attack. He is always in a set position directly behind the quarterback and three and one-half yards from the line of scrimmage.

Due to various splits of the offensive linemen, the tailback should line up even with and approximately two yards from the fullback. If the linemen are using minimum splits the tailback would be aligned with the inside hip of the tackle in front of him. He would be more in the gap between the tackle and guard if the linemen were using maximum splits.

A diagram of the alignments for the backs and ends in Right 100 formation is shown in Figure 2.6. For Left 100 formation the alignments would be the opposite.

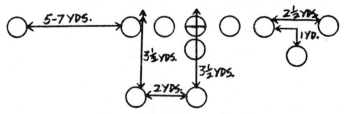

**Figure 2.6 Alignments for the
Backs and Ends in Right 100 Formation**

The Slot-Flex Formations

A variation of the short-slot is the slot-flex. The formation is still identified as the 100 formation. In Right 100 Flex the right end splits to a distance of seven yards. In Left 100 Flex the left end splits the same distance. (See Figures 2.7 and 2.8)

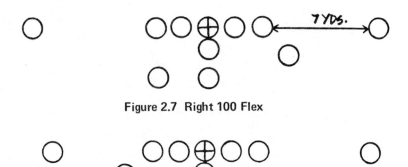

Figure 2.7 Right 100 Flex

Figure 2.8 Left 100 Flex

The Pro Set

The Pro Set formations are called Right 200 and Left 200. The slotback becomes a flanker to the side of the formation. The split of the flanker is from a minimum seven to a maximum ten yards from the end of his side. The end on the side of the formation will have a two yard split from the tackle, while the end away from the formation will maintain a minimum-five maximum-seven yard split. Unlike a true pro set, the fullback and the tailback will be in set positions rather than split. (See Figures 2.9 and 2.10)

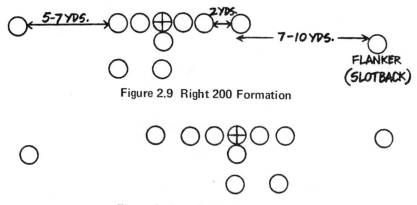

Figure 2.9 Right 200 Formation

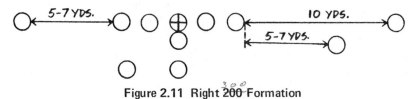

Figure 2.10 Left 200 Formation

The Wide-Slot Formations

The wide-slot formations are called Right 300 and Left 300. All positions maintain the same alignments and splits as the 100 and 200 formations except for the slotback and the end on the side of the formation. In Right 300 the right end is split ten yards from the tackle. The slot varies his split from five to seven yards. (See Figure 2.11)

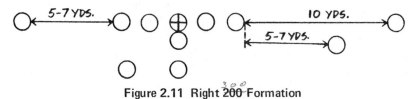

Figure 2.11 Right 200 Formation

Left 300 is the opposite. The minimum and maximum splits of the slotback are the same as an end away from the formation for the same reasons. The slotback should be split five yards to perform a seal block and seven yards to be a twin receiver with the end. A six yard split for the slot would be normal.

The Power I Formations

The power I formations are called Right 400 and Left 400. The formation is determined to the side of the halfback. (See Figures 2.12 and 2.13)

The slot in the 100 formations becomes the power back in the 400 formations. The tailback becomes the second man in the I

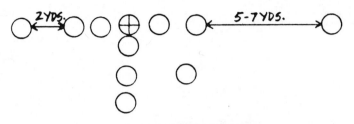

Figure 2.12 Right 400 Formation

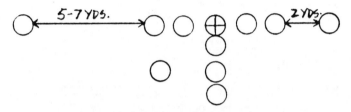

Figure 2.13 Left 400 Formation

alignment. The end on the side of the formation has a five to seven yard split. The 400 formation is the formation from which the shift will occur. The shift will be discussed in a later chapter.

Like the 100 formation, there is a variation to the 400 formation. It may be desirable in the case of a goal-line situation to have two tight ends. In this case the onside end, who is split, can be called to a tight end position. This is identified as 400 Tight. (See Figure 2.14)

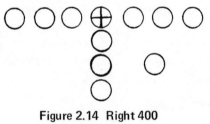

Figure 2.14 Right 400
Tight Formation

THE HOLE ATTACK

The Multiple Slot-T is an offense that attacks each hole or line opening. Being "freelance" (multiple) in nature, the use of series to identify the plays is not practical. The system of numbering the holes between linemen works very well to simplify the running game. The ends are numbered and pass zones are established to make the passing game easy to learn. The offense identifies the holes to the right as the even number holes, while the odd numbered holes are to the left. (See Figure 2.15)

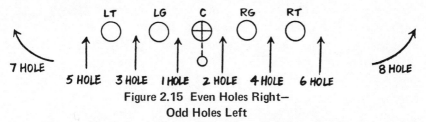

Figure 2.15 Even Holes Right—
Odd Holes Left

The path of the ball carrier varies slightly when running the football through these holes. An even or odd defensive alignment will be the primary reason for this deviation. A gap or stacked defensive alignment in the hole of the play that is called will usually require a check-off play at the line of scrimmage. (See Chapter 11 for use of audibles). Figure 2.16 indicates the numbers of the backs as they would be in a full backfield set.

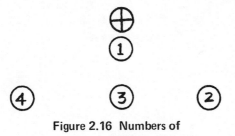

Figure 2.16 Numbers of
Backfield Personnel

The right halfback or #2 back and the left halfback or #4 back have five offensive alignments, depending on the formation. For example, the right halfback (#2) is the short slot in Right 100 formation, the flanker in Right 200 formation, the wide slot in Right 300 formation, the powerback in Right 400 formation, and the second man in the "I" alignment in Left 400 formation. The left halfback(#4) has the same alignments as the #2 back when the formations are reversed. The quarterback, who is #1, and the fullback, who is #3, have the stable alignment in the backfield. The left end is assigned the number seven and the right end the number eight, but their numbers are used only in the pass offense. The following formations have the personnel numbered along with the holes to show the basic frame of reference used in the Multiple Slot-T Offense for the purpose of calling and identifying the plays. (See Figures 2.17- 2.20)

The running play that is called directs one of the backs through one of the holes. The number of the back is given first, with the second number being the number of the hole. For example, play 24 directs the #2 back through the four hole. This play is a simple dive to the right side. Of course this play is not possible in all of the alignments of the #2 back, since he is not in the customary right halfback position some of the time. This merely is an example to show the basic method used in numbering the plays.

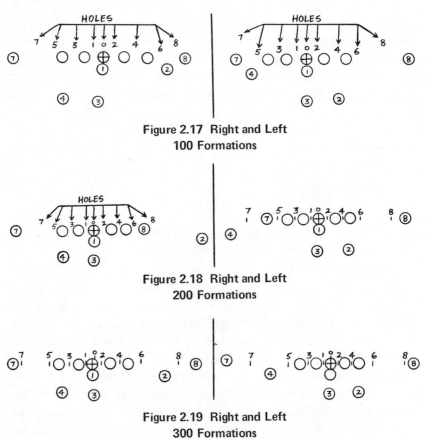

**Figure 2.17 Right and Left
100 Formations**

**Figure 2.18 Right and Left
200 Formations**

**Figure 2.19 Right and Left
300 Formations**

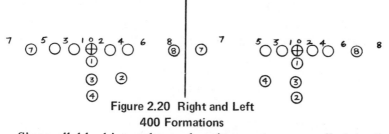

Figure 2.20 Right and Left
400 Formations

Since all blocking rules and assignments are applied to the hole in which the football is carried, it is important to communicate the type of block that is desired. This is accomplished by using terms like trap, power, isolation, option, etc., immediately following the number of the hole. For example, 46 Power communicates a power or double-team block in the six hole by the right tackle and slot, if the slot is there, or the right end if the slot is flanked. The play will not be confused with play 36, which is a rule block. If no blocking instruction follows the play that is called, the basic blocking rules are followed. Blocking rules are given in next chapter.

IDENTIFYING THE FORMATION AND PLAY

When the play is called in the huddle, the first directive of the quarterback is the formation (Right 1, Left 1, Right 2, Left 2, etc.). The next number is the number of the back, and the third number is the hole. For example, "Right 134" is the short slot formation (100) to the right, the "3 back" (fullback) carries the football through the four hole. (See Figure 2.21)

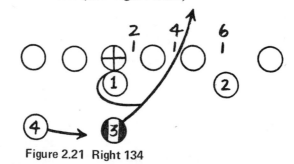

Figure 2.21 Right 134

Notice the number 34 takes the place of the two zeros in the 100 formation. The #4 back has a learned assignment for play 34.

All linemen and the #2 back will apply the four hole blocking rule. Since no blocking instructions follow the number of the play, the basic blocking rules are applied. The complete method of calling signals for the Multiple Slot-T offense is given in Chapter 11.

THE HUDDLE

It is significant that the ends, halfbacks, and center have a position in the huddle that will allow them to be in their proper alignments by the time the other members of the offense are set. One method of achieving this is to place the ends, halfbacks, and center in the front of an oval huddle, call the play to them and they leave the huddle. The play is repeated to the guards, tackles, and fullback. This method allows good timing between all positions of the offense. If the shift is employed the huddle is not significant, but the times when the shift is not used or certainly when the "2 minute offense" is in effect the huddle does become a factor. Figure 2.22 shows one type of huddle that provides easy access to the formations of the Multiple Slot-T.

Figure 2.22 The Huddle

If the halfbacks are to remain in an alignment between the offensive tackles they will take a step to the side to allow the linemen clearance, then will assume their alignments. The halfback who will be wider than the tackle will leave the huddle with the ends and center.

Chapter 3

Setting Up Blocking Rules for the Multiple Slot-T Attack

The types of blocks required by the Multiple Slot-T are not to be confused with the techniques of blocking. If some technique is mentioned it will be for the purpose of eliminating any misunderstanding of the terminology used by different coaches.

The various types of blocks the interior linemen will use include the drive, reach, cut-off, shoulder, fold, lead, trap, and power or double-team blocks for the running game. Pass protection blocking will include the aggressive method for play action and butt blocking for cup protection.

The ends and slot will use the double-team, shoulder, seal, crack, and butt blocks as their primary types of blocks. Straight shoulder, cross-body, and butt blocking are types of blocks the fullback and tailback will use.

All of these blocks are fundamental. The speed and direction of the defensive players are two factors that determine which techniques of blocking are used.

BASE BLOCKING FOR INTERIOR LINEMEN

Base blocking for the interior linemen refers to the basic rules they will follow in carrying out their assignment for a running play. The base or rule block will hold true against all common defenses. A stacked or stunting defense would require some adjustments in the base rule. These adjustments are called coaching points and are necessary to prevent confusion of the linemen. Switching from the rule block to the man block is one way to attack an unusual defensive alignment.

The lineman needs only to know which hole the ball carrier is going through to apply his blocking rule. If a blocking assignment other than a base rule block is used, the play that is called will communicate this to him. For example, play 32 is the #3 back through the two hole. Base blocking is used because no blocking instructions followed the number of the play. If play 42 Trap is called, the man block (which will be discussed in a later chapter) is used. Therefore the interior linemen learn a base block for each hole and learn a man block for some of the holes. Coaching points are used when encountering other blocking situations at the line of scrimmage.

Base Rule for the Center

The Base rules for the center in the order that he applies them are: 1. Over, 2. Gap Away, 3. Linebacker Away. Over refers to a defensive player in front of the center from the tip of one shoulder to the tip of the other shoulder, and either in the customary stance of the middle guard or in a linebacker stance. Figure 3.1 shows how the center's Base block would hold true for the two hole against three common defenses.

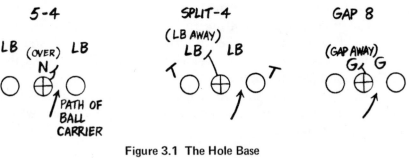

**Figure 3.1 The Hole Base
Blocking for the Center**

The Base rule for the Center holds true for all running plays with the exception of the traps, and they require a Man Block.

Base Blocking for the Guards

The Base rules for the guards in the order that they apply them are: 1. Gap, 2. Over, 3. Linebacker, 4. Fold. Gap refers to gap away. If an opponent is in the hole where the play is called, the guard treats that situation as gap away if the play is not changed at the line of scrimmage. The ball carrier, seeing this defensive alignment, will deviate his path slightly to the outside of the guard. The third rule of the guards refers to the nearest linebacker. The fourth rule for the guards is Fold and applies only when the play is wider than the two hole for the Right Guard or the one hole for the Left Guard. The Fold rule is used when it is not possible to block the linebacker to the inside by firing straight off the line of scrimmage. The guard never attempts to fold when a dive play is called. Figure 3.2 shows the center and the guards Base blocking against four common defenses.

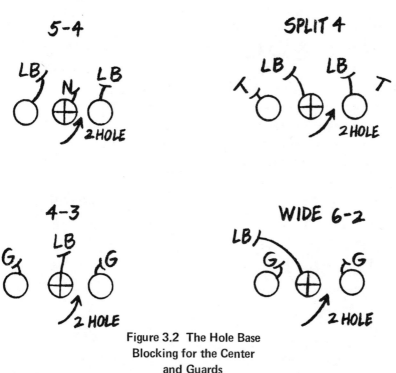

Figure 3.2 The Hole Base Blocking for the Center and Guards

Base Blocking for the Tackles

Base blocking for the tackles are Gap, Over, and Linebacker for holes one, two, three, and four, with the exception of the traps. Figures 3.3, 3.4, 3.5, and 3.6 show the Base blocking rules for the interior linemen for holes one, two, three, and four.

Center–Over, Gap, Linebacker Away
Guards–Gap, Over, Linebacker
Tackles–Gap, Over Linebacker

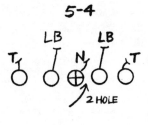

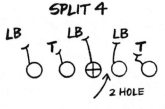

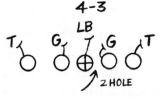

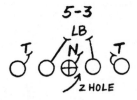

Figure 3.3 Two Hole Base Blocking
for Interior Linemen

Center–Over, Gap, Linebacker Away
Guards–Gap, Over, Linebacker, Fold
Tackles–Gap, Over, Linebacker

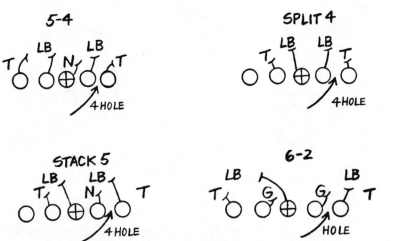

Figure 3.4 Four Hole Base
Blocking for Interior Linemen

Center–Over, Gap, Linebacker Away
Guards–Gap, Over, Linebacker
Tackles–Gap, Over, Linebacker

5-4

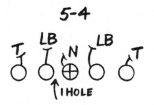

SPLIT 4

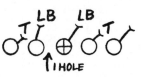

4-3

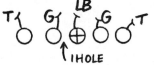

5-3

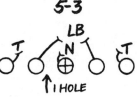

Figure 3.5 One Hole Blocking
for Interior Linemen

Center–Over, Gap, Linebacker Away
Guards–Gap, Over, Linebacker, Fold
Tackles–Gap, Over, Linebacker

5-4

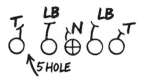

SPLIT 4

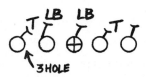

STACK 5

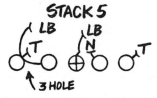

6-2

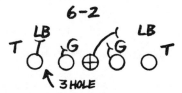

Figure 3.6 Three Hole Base
Blocking for Interior Linemen

The Base blocking rules for the interior linemen will hold true in most instances, but some defenses do place more personnel in an area than there are offensive personnel and thus prevent the usual match-ups. The Split-4 defense, for example, places four defensive players to the inside of the offensive tackles. If the blocking for play 32 (fullback through the two hole) was the same as shown in Figure 3.3 (Split-4 defense), the play would probably not be effective since the right tackle has a virtually impossible block. However, if play 42 Isolation were used the play could be highly successful. 42 Isolation utilizes the fullback as a lead blocker for the #4 (tailback) through the two hole. Under the Base rule the fullback would help the right tackle block the anchor tackle. However, a coaching point would be of greater value. The fullback could isolate the linebacker freeing the guard to help with the nearest defensive linemen. (See Figure 3.7.)

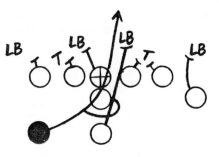

Figure 3.7 42 Isolation
Against a Split-4

The term "Isolation" following the play 42 communicates the desired block and enables the two hole attack to be effective against a defense that has the offense out-manned in an area. Isolation in the one, three, and four holes has similar results.

The Rule and Man blocking assignments for the interior linemen for holes five, six, seven, and eight will be given in the chapter dealing with the outside running game.

Blocking Assignments for the Ends

Since the ends play a tight-end and a split-end position, depending on the formation, their blocking assignments include both rule and man blocks. Being in a tight-end position will usually call for the rule block. The end's blocking assignment closely parallels the blocks of the short and wide slot in that the slot and the end on that side exchange blocking assignments in some situations. The slot and end will also double-team against some defensive alignments. The end must be aware of several situations and alignments to carry out his assignments effectively. The simplest part of the blocking assignments for the end to remember is that for all plays that are run away from him he is on the remove side, and he therefore gets to the running lane and blocks color. When the play is run to his side three circumstances dictate his assignment:

1. Whether the slot is inside him or flanked.
2. When he is the tight end.
3. When he is the split end.

The rule blocks for the ends have different terminology from the interior linemen since the defensive personnel can be spread over a larger area of the field. The rule for the end "linebacker as wide" is more of an area block which would include a linebacker in front of him, a monster outside the defensive end, a cornerback, or one of several defensive players, depending on which defensive alignment is used. A typical set of rules for the end would be (1) Inside, (2) Over, (3) Outside, and (4) Linebacker as wide. Inside would refer to any defensive player from the end's inside foot to the outside foot of the next offensive player, which would either be the slot or the tackle. Over is in front of the end, while outside would usually refer to the defensive end. When the Slot is in the short slot alignment (100 Formation) the end will ignore the "Inside" part of his rule because this will be the Slot's block.

Blocking Assignments for the Backs

When the Slot is in a short slot formation he will block Rule. When he is flanked or the wide slot his blocks will be Man. The fullback and tailback block Man exclusively. The Rule blocks for the ends and slot as well as the Man blocks for all the backs and ends will be given when each running play is discussed in the chapters that deal with the running game.

Checking Blocking Rules

One of the best methods of checking blocking rules to see if the rules will hold true for most defenses would be to use the Gap

8 defensive alignment as a control. If the rules hold up for the Gap 8 defense they will hold true for nearly all defensive alignments. Figure 3.8 shows the four hole rules for the strong side linemen and the slot against the 5-4, Split-4, 4-3, and Gap 8 defenses.

RULES

Center—Over, Gap Away, Linebacker Away
Guards—Gap, Over, Linebacker, Fold
Tackles—Gap, Over, Linebacker
Slot—Inside, Over, Linebacker as Wide
Right End—Inside, Over, Linebaker as Wide, Outside

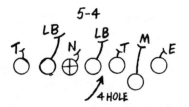
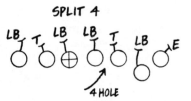

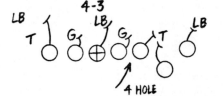
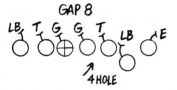

**Figure 3.8 Four Hole Blocking
Against 5-4, Split-4, 4-3,
and Gap 8**

Remember, the end ignores the "Inside" rule when the slot is inside him. All blocking rules apply effectively against the four defensive alignments shown in Figure 3.8.

Blocking assignments for all members of the offense are learned by the hole. Most of the blocks by the interior linemen are Rule blocks. The ends and slotback block both Rule and Man, while the fullback and tailback block Man. Trap, power, isolation, option, etc., along with the numbers of the play, give special meaning to bring about the desired blocking.

PART 2

Multiple Slot-T Running Game

Chapter 4

Coaching the Multiple Slot-T Inside Running Game Toward the Formation

The inside running game toward the formation includes three line openings: between the center and the strong guard, between the strong guard and the strong tackle, and between the strong tackle and the strong end. In formation Right these openings would be the two, four, and six holes. In formation Left the openings are the one, three, and five holes. Keep in mind that the number of the holes does not change when the formation changes. The even-numbered holes represent the strong side when formation Right is used. The odd-numbered holes are the strong side when formation Left is used.

Each play toward the formation has its counterpart when the opposite formation is used. For example, Right 34 is Left 33, Right 46 is Left 25, Right 42 trap is Left 21 trap, etc. Formation Right is usually used when teaching the plays. When the play is taught from formation Right the players are asked to give the number of the same play in Left formation. This is very easy to do and provides the players with an awareness of the overall offensive scheme.

If the flip-flop method were used only one-half as many plays would have to be learned, which would be fine for teams with considerable depth. For teams with a limited number of players, not flip-flopping is best. For example, if the left tackle had to be switched to right tackle and the four hole was called, all he would have to do is apply his three hole blocking to know his assignment.

The inside running game toward the formation will be discussed first from Right formation and then discussed for Left formation. The linemen apply their blocks according to the hole that is called. The backs who are not carrying the football have a learned assignment for each play.

THE TWO HOLE ATTACK FROM RIGHT FORMATION

The two hole is the area between the center and the right guard. The Multiple Slot-T attacks this area with the quarterback sneak, a wedge to the fullback, a trap to the tailback who is in a left halfback alignment, and an isolation play to the tailback with the fullback as the lead blocker. The quarterback sneak is called 12 sneak and the fullback wedge is called 32 wedge. These two plays involve "wedge" blocking by the linemen into the two hole. The tailback trap is called 42 trap while the tailback isolation play is called 42 isolation. The use of the words "trap" and "isolation" communicates the type of blocking we want from the linemen and the fullback. The 12 sneak and the 32 wedge plays can be run, without any adjustments, from any of the formations of the Multiple Slot-T. The 42 trap and the 42 isolation, because of the alignment of the tailback, are Right Formation play only. The two hole wedge plays will be discussed first.

Two Hole Wedge Plays

The 12 sneak is usually a short yardage play. The quarterback receives the snap and hesitates momentarily to allow the linemen to fire off the line, then drives into the two hole. The linemen will have minimum splits. If a defensive lineman is in the two hole the quarterback will either change the play or sneak over the outside hip of the right guard. All linemen are told to be very aggressive because it is a short yardage situation and the quarterback may be unsuccessful in the two hole and have to try one of the other holes. Figure 4.1 gives the two hole base blocking rules and shows how the rules apply to a gap 8 defense.

The set backs should be cautioned not to aid the quarterback's effort by pushing or driving him into the line of scrimmage.

RULES

Center—Over, Gap, Linebacker Away
Guards—Gap, Over, Linebacker
Tackles—Gap, Over, Linebacker
Slotback—Gap, Over, Linebacker
Weakside End—Running Lane
Strongside End—Inside, Running Lane
Fullback and Tailback—Straight Ahead

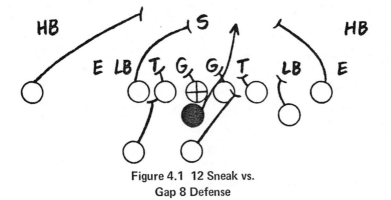

Figure 4.1 12 Sneak vs.
Gap 8 Defense

The fullback and tailback should blast into the four and three holles respectively. The interior linemen and slotback block their two hole base rule. The ends close inside to the running lane. The 12 sneak can be run from any of the formations. The opposite play of Right 112 sneak is Left 111 sneak. All rules and maneuvers are the same. (See Figure 4.2)

The base rules for the two hole in Figure 4.1 are the base rules for the one hole in Figure 4.2. The tight end in Figure 4.1 had "inside, running lane," as his two hole blocking rule. When the slotback is inside the tight end, which is the case of the 100 formation, the tight end ignores the inside part of his rule because that will be the slotback's block. In Figure 4.2, since the slot was not present, the end blocks his inside rule.

Right 32

Play 32 is the other two hole wedge to the side of the formation. The linemen and the slotback will block their two hole

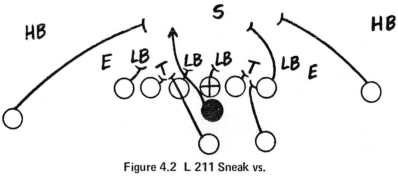

Figure 4.2 L 211 Sneak vs.
Split-4 Defense

base rules. The fullback, who is the ball carrier, has to read the hole for a gapped defensive player or anything that might make his path through the hole deviate. When the fullback gets to the hole he may need to make an adjustment to his running lane. Figure 4.3 gives the two hole base rules and shows how the play is run against a 5-4 defense.

   Center—Over, Gap Away, Linebacker Away
   Guards—Gap, Over, Linebacker
   Tackles—Gap, Over, Linebacker
   Slotback—Gap, Over, Linebacker
   Strong End—Inside, Running Lane
   Weak End—Running Lane
   Tailback—Sweep Strong

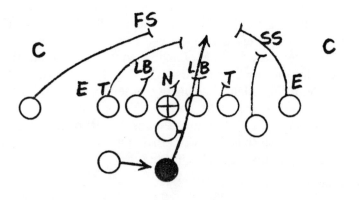

Figure 4-3 Right 132 vs.
5-4 Defense

The tight end ignores the inside rule, because the slotback is there and blocks running lane. The strong end, because of his alignment, has executed a cut-off block on the defensive end.

The quarterback opens to the side of the two hole by planting his strong side foot at 6 o'clock and parallel to the line of scrimmage. The left foot (if in formation right) pivots to a parallel position. The back must be straight to prevent the quarterback's head from colliding with the near side of the fullback. The football is handled with both hands and a basic hand-off technique is executed. This is done by placing the ball in the stomach of the fullback, removing the hand nearest to the fullback first, and finishing the hand-off with the other hand. The quarterback finishes his assignment by placing his right hand on his top hip (farthest from the line of scrimmage), grasps his right wrist with the left hand, and fakes a keep or bootleg to the strong side. Keep in mind that the play is being discussed for Right formation. Formation Left would be the opposite of this when mentioning right and left foot or right and left hand.

The tailback opens toward the formation with one drop step toward the top of the backfield, sprints parallel to the line of scrimmage, and turns downfield when he gets outside the tight end. For Left formation the play is 31 and can be run from any formation. (See Figure 4.4)

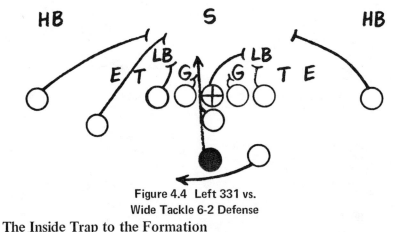

Figure 4.4 Left 331 vs.
Wide Tackle 6-2 Defense

The Inside Trap to the Formation

In Right formation the inside trap is 42 trap while in Left formation it is 21 trap. The interior linemen have a trap rule that is determined by the defensive alignment. Whether the defense is an odd or even alignment is the usual method for determining the blocking rules.

The center always blocks away from the hole. The guard away from the hole does the trapping. For example, if the two hole trap is called the guard away is the left guard. The guard away or the weak-side guard does the trapping on all trap plays. Figure 4.5 gives the trap rules and Figure 4.6 shows how they apply to four common defenses.

Weakside End—Running Lane
Weakside Tackle—Cut-off, Linebacker
Weakside Guard—Trap first to show
Center—Over, Seal
Strong Guard—Odd Defense—Double-Team with Center
                Even Defense—Linebacker, turn out on next
                      man
Strong Tackle—Linebacker, Gap Away
Slotback—Gap, Over, Linebacker
Strong End—Inside, Over, Cut-off, Running Lane

Figure 4.5 The Inside Trap Rules

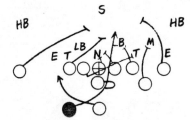

R142 Trap vs. 5-4

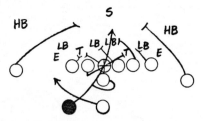

R242 Trap vs. Split-4

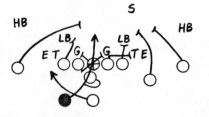

R342 Trap vs. Wide 6-2

Figure 4.6 Trap Against the 5-4, Split-4, 6-2, and 4-3 Defense

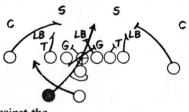

R242 Trap vs. 4-3

For 42 trap the weak tackle has a cut-off block first. If his alignment gives him the advantage of the cut-off simply by firing off the line of scrimmage, he does not need to be concerned with this defensive lineman to his outside. The tackle can go to his second rule of blocking the linebacker. However, if the weak tackle does not have the advantage of alignment, where a defensive lineman is inside, he will have to execute a reach block to cut off that defensive lineman. The center will most likely be seal blocking that same lineman, but that is fine since it is difficult for the center to seal between the guard and the tackle. There is usually too much penetration by the defensive lineman. This is certainly the case of a split-4 defense where both anchor tackles are pinching to the inside.

The weak guard pulls and traps the first man to show, which in most cases is the first defensive lineman past the center. The guard finds his trap block on the first step of his pulling maneuver. A stunting linebacker may meet him before the trap block. If this happens the guard is to cut the linebacker down if possible.

The center blocks over if an odd defense is used, and he gets a double-team block from the strong guard. If the defense is in an even alignment the strong guard has to read the following alignments. If there is one linebacker the guard blocks him. If there are two linebackers the guard blocks the far one. If there are no linebackers the strong guard will turn out on the next defensive lineman. The strong guards need to be reminded of their inside trap rules for Right and Left formations often, until they are able to read the rules by themselves.

The strong tackle blocks near linebacker and gap away. Stunts of various sorts will require some coaching points to the trap rules. When the one hole trap is used the blocking of the linemen is the opposite of the two hole trap.

The Backfield Action for Right 42 Trap

The path of the ball carrier and the footwork of the quarterback varies slightly, depending on whether the defense has an odd or even alignment. In an even defensive alignment the path of the ball carrier is in the zero hole, while against an odd defense his path is the two hole. This deviation in the path of the ball carrier will not affect the number of the play.

The quarterback reverses out, always opening to the strong side, then pivots into approximately a 270 degree position to execute the hand-off. His first step from a parallel position would be made with the foot that is toward the strong side. In Right formation this step is with the right foot and is made to a four o'clock position. (The quarterback is facing twelve o'clock before the snap.) A clockwise pivot is made off the right foot to the 270 degree position. The quarterback would be facing the inside hip of the weak-side tackle if the tackle were still there. The hand-off is made to the right side of the tailback. The quarterback finishes his maneuver by moving to the weak side with a bootleg fake. For Left formation the footwork described above would be the opposite.

The fullback goes behind the tailback toward the defensive end on the weak side, then turns for downfield blocking. The tailback, who is the ball carrier, steps with the inside foot at two o'clock for an even defense and three o'clock for an odd defense. He then bows his path slightly for the correct path to the hole. After the hand-off he will turn downfield off the trap block of the weak guard. The slotback will block his two hole rule or downfield if in another formation. The slot is also used for weak and strong side motion. The companion play for Right 42 trap is Left 21 trap. The blocking rules for the linemen alternate where the right guard is now executing the trap block. (See Figure 4.7)

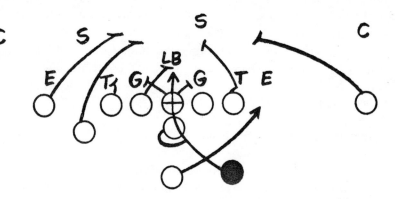

Figure 4.7 Left 21 Trap vs.
6-1 Defense

The Two Hole Isolation from Right Formation

The two hole isolation play from Right formation involves wedge blocking or basic rule blocking for the interior linemen. The fullback is used for the isolation block. The play in Right formation is 42 isolation. Using the fullback as a lead blocker into the two hole provides an equal match-up when the defensive alignment is stacked inside. An example would be a split-4 or split-6 defense. The 42 isolation can be run from any of the Right formation alignments. When the #4 back is in the set position the action of the quarterback is identical to 42 trap. In Right 400 formation, where the #4 back is the second man in the I alignment, the quarterback opens toward the formation and plants the strong side foot at six o'clock, then allows the fullback to clear. He then gives the football to the second man through, which is the tailback. Figure 4.8 shows Right 42 isolation from both the set positions and the I positions.

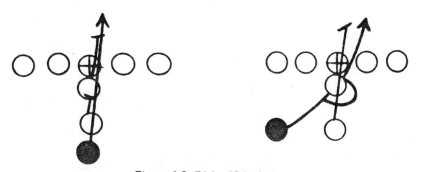

Figure 4.8 Right 42 Isolation
from Set and I Alignments

The fullback will blast into the two hole to clear for the tailback. Against an odd defensive alignment the fullback will usually be helping the strong guard. In an even defense, such as the split-4 and split-6, the fullback will have a Man block. This will be the strong side linebacker.

THE FOUR HOLE ATTACK FROM RIGHT FORMATION

The four hole attack from Right formation includes four plays to attack the opening between the strong guard and strong tackle. These plays are a strong side belly, a tailback isolation, a dive, and a tailback cross-buck.

The Strong Side Belly

The strong side belly is the first phase of a valuable series in the Multiple Slot-T. The fullback hitting into the four hole is a highly successful play. This action begins the strong side option, is used in the outside trap to the weak side, and is used in play action passes. Figure 4.9 shows the strong side belly, which is play 34 in Right formation, against a split-4 defense. The four hole blocking rules are also given.

Weak End—Running Lane
Weak Tackle—Cut-Off, Linebacker
Weak Guard—Gap, Over, Linebacker
Center—Over, Gap Away, Linebacker Away
Strong Guard—Gap, Over, Linebacker, Fold
Strong Tackle—Gap, Over, Linebacker
Slotback—Inside, Over, Linebacker
Strong End—Inside, Over, Linebacker, Outside

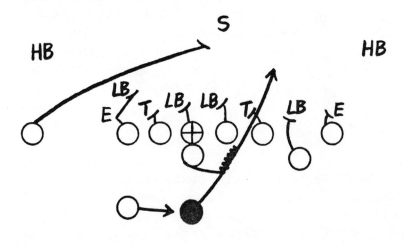

Figure 4.9 R134 vs. Split-4
Defense

Figure 4.10 shows three other formations from which Right 34 or Left 33 can be run. They are run against the 6-2, 5-4, and gap 8 defenses to show how the blocking rules apply.

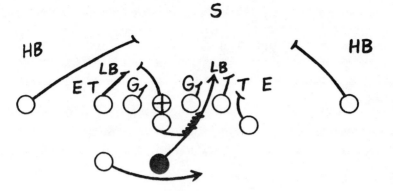

R1 Flex 34 vs. 6-2 Defense

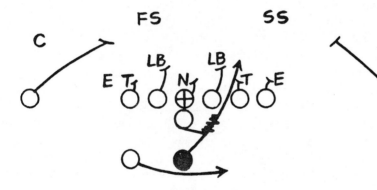

R234 vs. 5-4 Defense

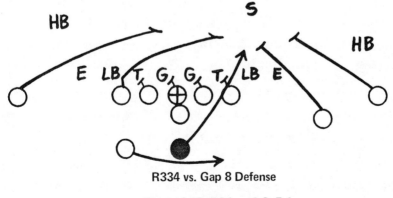

R334 vs. Gap 8 Defense

Figure 4.10 R34 vs. 6-2, 5-4
and Gap 8 Defenses

When using 300 formation against a gap 8 defense, the blocking rules will not provide a blocker for the left linebacker since the slot is split. This is provided the linebacker doesn't loosen to adjust to the wide slot. The four hole isolation to the tailback using the fullback as a lead blocker would be an effective offensive maneuver to attack this defense. The strong guard doesn't have a fold situation against any of the defenses shown, and seldom will on the strong side unless an overshifted defense is used. The fold rule is used considerably on the weak side attack.

The Backfield Action for Right 34

The quarterback reverses out, opening to the weak side. His pivot will allow him to meet the fullback as soon as possible and approximately two yards in the backfield. The quarterback will ride the fullback into the line, handing off as late as he can. If the belly option is the called play, the action is the same except the quarterback will keep the football and proceed to the option area. The belly hand-off and the belly option are predetermined. The quarterback does not read the defense. For Right formation the quarterback reverses out to his left, pivots on the right foot and swings the left foot around to a four o'clock position before placing the foot on the ground. He extends the football into the stomach of the fullback as he brings his right foot into shoulder width position and even with the left foot. His next footwork is a quick shuffle step toward the line of scrimmage as he rides the fullback. The quarterback will extend the football beyond his left side toward the line of scrimmage, then hand to the fullback or in the option return it to a position in front of him. In R34, after the hand-off the quarterback continues down the line and fakes the option pitch to the tailback. The reverse out instead of the open out by the quarterback is used to hold the linebackers for an instant. This reverse out also provides an extra step for the tailback to get in position for the pitch when the option is used. The fullback will read the block of the strong tackle as he hits into the line. The tackle has an option block when a defensive lineman is over him. The fullback also will deviate his path against some defensive alignments that place an opponent in the four hole. The tailback takes one step toward the top of the backfield to gain depth of about four yards from the line of scrimmage. He then sprints to place himself four yards in front of the quarterback when the option is used. The slotback and linemen block their four hole rules. The companion play to R34 is L33. All blocking rules and backfield maneuvers are reversed to adapt to the opposite formation. Figure 4.11 shows the belly toward Left formation.

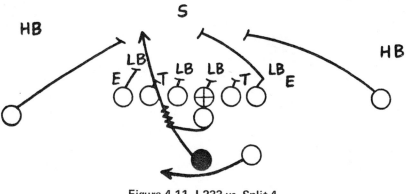

Figure 4.11 L233 vs. Split-4 Defense

Notice the strong side end ignored his inside blocking rule for the four hole when the slotback was inside him in Figure 4.8, but applied his inside rule when the slot was outside him as shown in Figure 4.10.

Right 44 Isolation

The four hole isolation play is very effective against a stacked defense. The fullback leads through the four hole for 44 isolation and the three hole for 23 isolation. The interior linemen will use their basic four hole blocking rules unless a coaching point is needed. Figure 4.12 shows the 44 isolation against a stack-five defense to the strong side.

Running the isolation from a pro alignment spreads the defense a little but still resembles a power attack by using the fullback for the isolation. The base blocking rules apply very well for the stacked five alignment as shown in Figure 4.12. The wide receivers block running lane while the tight end blocks his base rule of inside, over, outside, which in this case is "outside" the defense end. The strong tackle's rule is gap, over linebacker, therefore his "over" block will take care of the defensive tackle on

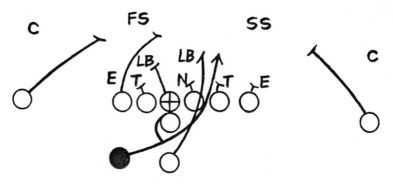

**Figure 4.12 R244 Isolation vs.
Stacked Five Defense**

his outside shoulder. The strong guard blocks gap, over, line-backer, and fold. The "gap" block on the nose man provides the strong guard with an excellent angle block at the point of attack. The center blocks the "linebacker away" part of his base rule. The weak side guard has a gap rule block while the weak side tackle, because of his alignment, has a cut-off block on the end away. The fullback will lead into the four hole and block the first to show, which most likely is the linebacker. The tailback does nothing deceptive. He merely drives into the four hole on the heels of the fullback. The tailback's first step should be parallel to the line of scrimmage simply to form a base to drive into the four hole.

The quarterback reverses out by opening to the weak side. For 44 isolation he will plant his left foot at 6 o'clock, pointed toward the top of the backfield. He will pivot 180 degrees on the right foot. The football will be extended more than usual to execute the hand-off to the tailback. The emphasis to all three backs is quickness. The fullback blasts into the four hole, followed closely by the tailback, and the quarterback steps out to make the hand-off as quickly as possible. After the hand-off the quarterback fakes a bootleg toward the strong side. If the defense is using a five man front of some type, 44 isolation from 200 formation would be more effective than from 100 formation. The R144 isolation (the isolation from the short-slot formation) would probably result in the defense inverting the strong safety and jamming the four hole. Against an even defense R144 isolation would be more effective. This utilizes the slotback as an inside blocker, since most even alignments result in 8 men being near the line of scrimmage.

Of course, the scouting report will determine which formation 44 isolation will be run from when preparing the game plan. The Left formation play for 44 isolation is 23 isolation. Figure 4.13 shows Left 123 isolation against a split-4 defense. All base blocking rules are used. with the slotback blocking gap, over, or linebacker.

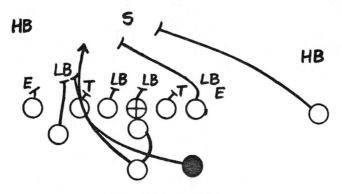

**Figure 4.13 L123 Isolation vs.
Split-4 Defense**

In Figure 4.13, the fullback may have to help the slotback with the linebacker. A common stunt for a split-4 defense is to pinch the anchor tackle to the inside and deal the linebacker on a common "X" stunt. This should not hurt L123 isolation. The fullback blocks inside-out on the isolation and therefore should be able to pick up the linebacker. Figure 4.14 shows how the tailback isolation in the three hole and four hole is run from the 100 flex, 300, and 400 formations.

The quarterback does not reverse out for 44 isolation when the power I formation is used. He opens to the four hole and makes the hand-off to the tailback as soon as the fullback clears. The power back, who is the slotback, blocks his four hole rule as though he were in a slot alignment, but he knows the right end is split and therefore has to assume the end's block. If the slotback executed his regular block, which would be the linebacker, and let the fullback kick the end out, the defensive end could close to the inside and jam the four hole. The fullback has to kick the linebacker but is actually blocking color from the inside out.

As the pattern of the Multiple Slot-T indicates, a few plays are run from several formations. With the addition of motion the

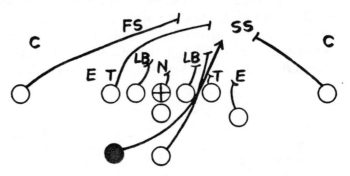

R1 Flex 44 Isolation vs. 5-4
Defense

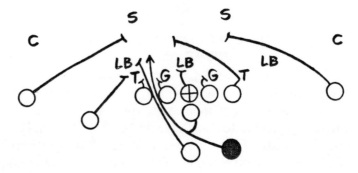

L323 Isolation vs. 4-3 Defense

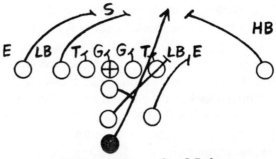

R444 Isolation vs. Gap 8 Defense

Figure 4.14

offense becomes very versatile. It certainly is impossible to run all of the plays in the course of one football game. In fact, research would narrow the number of running plays most teams use in a game to perhaps a dozen or less, with fewer passes than running plays. The Multiple Slot-T provides a repertoire from which the game plan can be derived without adding special plays each week but merely concentrating on certain aspects of something that is already there.

The Three and Four Hole Cross-Bucks

The three and four hole base blocking rules are used for the cross-bucks. The backfield action, with good faking, can provide a great deal of deception and freeze some defensive people momentarily to allow the linemen some blocking advantages. The play is called Right 44 X and Left 23 X. The "X" represents the fullback and tailback crossing action. Figure 4.15 shows the cross-buck to the side of the formation.

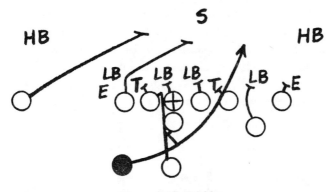

Figure 4.15 R144 vs.
Split-4 Defense

If the defensive alignment is an even with the normal eight people near the line of scrimmage, the short slot formation (100) is the only formation from which the cross-buck can be run effectively. There is no isolation block to match up with the defense. Any of the other formations can be used against a five man alignment with the exception of a true monster defense.

The fullback, for the cross-buck, hits into the nearest weak side hole, which would be a play 31 fake in Right formation and a play 32 fake in Left formation. The fake of the fullback is essential. He does not touch the football during the fake. The football is faked to the fullback and removed just before he gets near the ball. The closer the near shoulders of the fullback and the quarterback (to remove daylight) the better the fake, provided there is no contact. The fullback will complete his fake by staying bent and grasping each elbow with the opposite hand.

The tailback cuts off the far hip of the fullback with a slightly bowed path to the hole. After the hand-off he squares into the hole and straight downfield before attempting to break to the outside.

The quarterback opens to the weak side by placing the weak side foot at 6 o'clock and parallel to the line of scrimmage. A 90 degree pivot with the strong foot will place him in a position to fake the football to the fullback. His back must remain straight with his knees bent slightly. The back is straight to allow the fullback to be close without head or shoulder contact between the fullback and the quarterback. The football is faked to the fullback before the fullback actually arrives. The quarterback then steps back to the strong side with the top foot to a 4 or 5 o'clock position to make the hand-off to the tailback. At the same time he brings the other foot to a parallel position to form a normal base. After the hand-off the quarterback fakes a strong side bootleg. The opposite of R44X is L23X. Figure 4.16 shows the cross-buck to the left side against an odd defense.

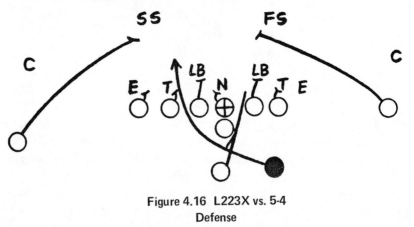

Figure 4.16 L223X vs. 5-4
Defense

44X and 23X are not run from the 400 (power I formations) as far as being strong side plays. These two plays are weak side plays for the 400 formation since the power I strong and weak side is determined by the power back side, not the tight end side.

Each coach has his own ideas concerning how he would like to execute hand-offs, fakes, bellies, etc. The Multiple Slot-T involves having both hands on the football when executing hand-offs and fakes. Some coaches prefer executing the cross-buck, for example, by giving the fullback a hand fake, having the football in the other hand and hidden from the defense by the quarterback's body. The football would then be handed to the tailback by one hand. There are several advantages to keeping both hands on the football. Most high school quarterbacks do not have hands as good as older quarterbacks. Contact with members of the backfield or penetrating defensive people isn't as likely to jar the football loose, and few adjustments in the quarterback's ball handling would be necessary for wet weather. These are a few of the advantages of keeping both hands on the football as much as possible.

The Dives

The only formation in which the dive play is a part of the inside running game toward the formation is Right or Left 400. This formation has a set back in a dive position on the side of the formation. Regardless of the formation, when a set back is aligned behind an offensive tackle a dive can be run. The two dives are R24 and L43. Four or three hole base blocking is used, with one exception. When 24 dive or 43 dive is called the guard never fold blocks because of the quickness of the play. If a fold situation occurs on defense the play will either be changed with an audible at the line of scrimmage or the ball carrier will deviate his path and the guard will block gap. The word "dive" is given after the number of the play to remind the guard not to fold. The defensive alignment will determine the path of the dive back. Generally, against an even defense the back will dive straight at the offensive tackle. In an odd defense the path is over guard. Figure 4.17 shows Right 424 dive against an odd and an even defense.

The quarterback has to realize there is an extra step in his footwork for the dive against the even defense. Another inside blocker can be obtained for the dive by using the 400 tight formation, in which the end is not split. The dive should be quick enough to go past the defensive tackle in the wide tackle 6-2.

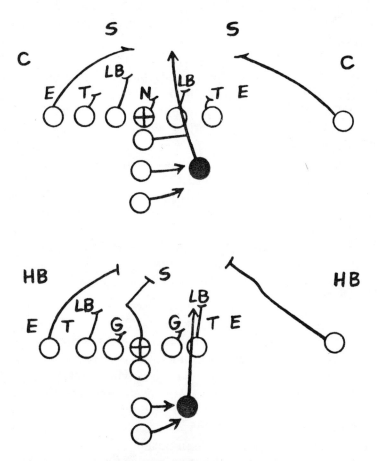

**Figure 4.17 R424 Dive vs.
5-4 and 6-2 Defenses**

A coaching point could be inserted at this time. In a wide tackle 6 or any defense with a three deep secondary, seldom is rotation in the secondary used to compensate for the long motion of a back. If the linebacker takes the strong side motion of a back the strong tackle will see this and is instructed to block the nearest man. In this case it would be the defensive tackle who would open the dive hole. A quick adjustment by the defense may close that hole, but some gain has been made. How the defense handles strong and weak side motion by the tailback and the slotback is vital when planning how to attack the defense.

THE OFF-TACKLE ATTACK TOWARD THE FORMATION

The off-tackle area toward the formation is between the strong tackle and the strong end. In Right formation this is the six hole and in Left formation the five hole. Generally, the formation for the six or five hole attack requires the maximum number of blockers we can have in that area. The formation that provides this is the 100 or short slot. The two plays in this area are a fullback slant and a tailback power. Sometimes one or both of these plays can be run from the 100 flex, 200, 300, and 400 formations. This depends on the number of defensive personnel in that area. The fullback slant is R36 and L35. The tailback power is R46 power and L25 power. The blocking for the fullback slant is Rule while the tailback power involves an off-tackle power block.

The Fullback Slant

Generally, R36 and L35 can be more effective if run from the 100 formation. Even with a 5-4 defense where the corner is outside, the defensive tackle on the strong side has an outside eye alignment on the strong tackle. This gives the defensive tackle an alignment advantage. The backfield action for the slant is not deceptive since it involves a simple drive-out by the quarterback. This makes it difficult for the strong tackle to reach block the defensive tackle. With the short slot formation the defense will have to invert a safety or use a monster, linebacker, or some such alignment that will place a defensive player near the slot. This would probably cause the defensive tackle to close down a little, which would create a one-on-one situation for the strong tackle, slotback, and tight end. Some offenses attack the off-tackle area by employing the "Tom and Charlie" blocks. (The end blocks down and the tackle kicks out.) The time when this is generally used is when the defensive tackle has an advantage on the offensive tackle by virtue of his alignment. If a defensive tackle is in this area and he is physically equal to the offensive tackle, that area cannot be attacked consistently with "Tom and Charlie" blocking. Power blocking, which involves a double team block on that defensive tackle, would be more effective. The Multiple Slot-T will not usually challenge a wide tackle 6-2 defense with the fullback slant. Figures 4.18, 4.19, and 4.20 give the six and five hole blocking rules and the plays against common defenses that have a defensive tackle over or inside the strong tackle.

Weak-Side End—Running Lane
Weak Tackle—Cut-Off, Running Lane
Weak Guard—Over, Linebacker
Center—Over, Gap Away, Linebacker Away
Strong Guard—Gap, Over, Linebacker
Strong Tackle—Gap, Over, Linebacker
Strong End—Over, Outside
Slotback—Gap, Over, Linebacker, Safety

**Figure 4.18 Six and Five Hole
Slant Blocking Rules**

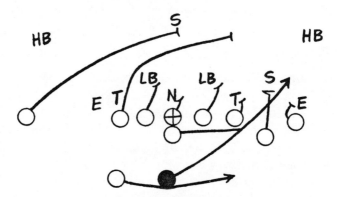

**Figure 4.19 R136 vs. 5-4 Defense
with Inverted Safety**

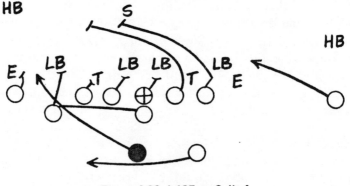

**Figure 4.20 L135 vs. Split-4
Defense**

The quarterback opens to the strong side and takes the football to the fullback. The quarterback's maneuver is similar to a dive to that side in that he must move down or slightly into the line. After the hand-off the quarterback fakes a keeper to the strong side. The fullback is instructed to run a straight path to the six or five hole. Considerable practice is necessary for the fullback to attain this. There is a natural tendency for backs to move laterally and then cut up the hole. The purpose of the straight path is to get into the hole as quickly as possible. The tailback, if not in strong or weak motion, takes a drop step with his strong side foot toward the top of the backfield, then sprints to the strong side. He will keep approximately four yards from the line of scrimmage. The motion of the tailback that is mentioned above is used to get the defense to move. For example, when the tailback goes in motion to the weak side, if the secondary rolls to that side, the off-tackle hole may open more. This would make 36 and 35 slants easier to run. The motion of the tailback and the slotback will be discussed in the chapter dealing with "Attacking the Defense."

The only other formation in which the slant is effective would be from 400 tight. Here the power back isolates the off-tackle hole. (See Figure 4.21)

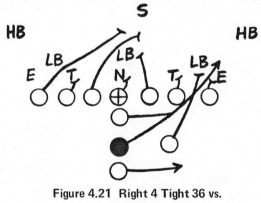

**Figure 4.21 Right 4 Tight 36 vs.
5-3 Defense**

The Power Off-Tackle

The power off-tackle, which is Right 46 and Left 25, utilizes a power or double team block at the point of attack. The play employs some of the single wing concept: a double team block, a kick-out block on the defensive end by the fullback, and a pulling guard to lead into the hole. The 46 and 25 powers can attack the off-tackle hole when the defensive alignment places a tackle outside the offensive tackle. This would be the defensive player that would be double-teamed. The tailback is the ball carrier. Figure 4.22 gives the blocking rules for the power off-tackle.

Weak End—Running Lane
Weak Tackle—Cut-Off, Running Lane
Weak Guard—Pull
Center—Over, Seal
Strong Guard—Gap, Over, Linebacker
Strong Tackle—Gap, Over, Linebaker
Strong End—Inside, Near Halfback

**Figure 4.22 Blocking Rules for
the Power Off-Tackle**

The weak side end and tackle have standard off side blocking rules. However, if a defensive lineman is between the weak tackle and weak guard, the weak tackle tries to cut him off. The weak side guard pulls and is instructed to knock down any color that shows before reaching the off-tackle hole. As the pulling guard turns into the hole he blocks color. If no color shows he seals back to the inside. Actually, if the assignment of the linemen and slotback are carried out, the pulling guard will be sealing a linebacker who "quick reads" the flow or a safety who is coming up to make the play.

The center blocks "over, seal" as his rules. He is sealing for the pulling guard. In a split-4 defense or an alignment that places a defensive lineman outside the pulling guard, the seal block by the center is difficult to execute. This is why the weak side tackle is instructed to reach the inside gap to at least stop the penetration of this defensive lineman. An aggressive defensive linemen who is closing to the inside rapidly can get to the tailback before he reaches the off-tackle hole. The strong guard has a standard rule block of gap, over, and linebacker. When his rule reads linebacker, if he can cut the linebacker off it would free the pulling guard to block someone else.

The strong tackle has a standard or base blocking rule, but he must realize the double-team block and execute a post block instead of reaching the defensive tackle. The strong tackle will have a double-team block with the slotback or possibly the strong end anytime the defensive tackle is in an "over" position, which is head-up, inside eye, or outside eye. The slotback has an inside and over rule. He will double-team with the strong tackle when the inside rule applies and double team with the strong end when the over rule applies. The slotback is the drive blocker with the tackle, and the post blocker with the end. Moving the defensive player who is being double-teamed is vital to the success of the power play.

The strong end blocks inside the near halfback. In the two other inside holes (one or two and three or four) if the slot was inside him the end ignored his inside rule. This is not true for the power. The end will block the inside rule whether the slot is there or not. This allows for the double-team the slotback has with either the strong tackle or strong end. If there is no defensive player to the inside the strong end will block the nearest defensive halfback, who may be the strong safety or a cornerback.

The fullback blocks the defensive end. If the defensive end has closed to the inside and is in the hole, the fullback blocks the outside half of the defensive end with a body block. If the defensive end "boxes" (steps across and turns to the inside), which is ideal, the fullback uses a shoulder block, keeping his head toward the hole. Figures 4.23, 4.24, 4.25, and 4.26 show 46 and 25 power against several common defenses.

The power can be run with the strong end split or with the slotback flanked (Figure 4.25) but it would be giving up too much to the inside to run the power with the end and the slot split, which is the 300 formations.

There are two backfield executions for 46 and 25 power. One is when the backs are in set positions and the other is when the backs are in the "I" alignment. Most of the time the play will be run from set positions to utilize the maximum number of blockers.

In 100 and 200 formations the quarterback pivots on his strong side foot and plants the weak side foot at seven o'clock for Right formation and five o'clock for Left formation (the quarterback is facing 12 o'clock before the snap). The pitch is made to the tailback in the same motion as the step. There is a

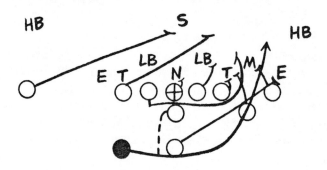

Figure 4.23 R146 Power vs.
5-4 Monster Defense

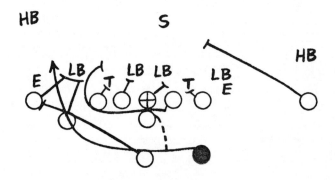

Figure 4.24 L125 Power vs.
Split-4 Defense

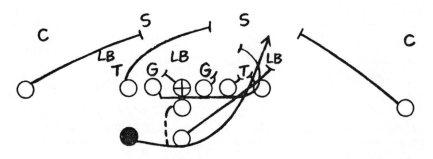

Figure 4.25 R246 vs.
4-3 Pro Defense

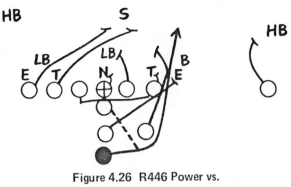

Figure 4.26 R446 Power vs.
5-3 Defense

continuous motion of ball, pivot, and step after the quarterback receives the snap. Between the snap and pitch the quarterback rotates his hands under the football and pitches it "fat" and at chest level to the tailback. The quarterback does not put any spiral or significant velocity on the ball. The quarterback is not off-balance at this point. After the pitch the quarterback steps toward the defensive end on the weak side with the strong side foot. He finishes up with two or three steps to the weak side with very little fake. The effect is to get the defensive end used to seeing the quarterback come his way with the play going in the opposite direction. The end is more or less being shown that the quarterback is getting clear of any collisions. The power play might be a little more effective if the quarterback were to pitch and team with the fullback on the defensive end on the strong side. However, the above method is desired for two reasons: the safety of the quarterback, and using the quarterback as a blocker for the slotback reverse that is run off the action of the power.

The first motion of the tailback is to pivot on the weak side foot and rotate his body to the direction of the strong side (similar to a pulling guard). He executes a drop step with the strong side foot toward the top of the backfield to gain an additional half-yard distance from the line of scrimmage. He brings his hands up to stomach level with the palms facing each other. From this position he can turn his thumbs out for the low pitch and turn them in for the high pitch. He must take the pitch in full stride with no hesitation to be able to reach the hole with good timing. The following sequence of steps will explain the footwork of the tailback for Right formation: pivot on left foot and open shoulders toward strong side . . . plant right foot parallel to line of scrimmage . . . bring hands up and step with left foot still parallel to line . . . right-left-right . . . drive off the right foot into hole. If the fullback has blocked out on the end the tailback turns upfield. If the fullback has to hook the end the tailback can veer outside, but does not go any deeper in the backfield to get outside.

From the power I formation the pitch is executed differently. Here the quarterback opens to the strong side and pitches to the tailback on his first step. The ball still floats, similar to the pitch from the set positions. The quarterback then moves toward the weak side even though the reverse is not run from this formation. The tailback receives the pitch similar to the set position. He takes one less step with each foot before turning upfield into the hole. An advantage of the pitch from 400 formation is that the tailback can get to the hole more quickly. A disadvantage is that a good double-team block would be hard to make. The power back in the I alignment isolates in the off-tackle hole. It may be to help the tackle or to block a linebacker.

Chapter 5

Coaching the Multiple Slot-T Outside Running Game Toward the Formation

The outside running game toward the formation will be discussed from one formation at a time, with and without motion of the backs. This will show all the possibilities of the outside running game of the Multiple Slot-T. Certainly all of these maneuvers will not be used in the course of one game. One of the good features of the offense is its flexibility in fitting into the game plan. Instead of teaching new things each week to attack the opponent you face, you are merely focusing on those parts of the offense that will give your opponent the most trouble. Regardless of the formation or whether motion is used or not, the rules that are established for the outside running game to the strong side are followed. The formation and motion merely means the offensive player will execute his assignment from several different alignments. There are only a few situations where offensive personnel have to swap assignments because of their alignment.

The blocking assignments for the outside running game involve man blocks for the backs and the ends rather than rule blocks. For the inside running game the defensive alignment has to place a man within a small area, up or down, and on or off the line—therefore rule blocking is easy to apply. However, when ends and backs are aligned in various positions and motion is used, defensive personnel also move. Using a man assignment for the outside areas is much simpler than applying rules. Also, rules that would apply to all defenses would be difficult to write.

The outside running game toward the formation includes a belly option, a lead option, and in one formation a quick-pitch. The man blocking assignments for each of these plays will be given first and then the play will be discussed from each of the formations. Motion of the tailback or slotback will also be shown for some situations. Figure 5.1 gives the blocking assignments for the belly option.

Weak End—Running Lane
Weak Tackle—Cut-Off, Remove or Running Lane
Weak Guard—Gap, Over, Linebacker
Center—Over, Gap Away, Linebacker Away
Strong Guard—Gap, Over, Linebacker
Strong Tackle—Gap, Over, Linebacker
Strong End—First man in secondary

**Figure 5.1 Blocking Assignments
for the Belly Option**

From the weak side end through the strong side tackle base blocking rules are used. The strong tackle will reach block to gain outside leverage on the defensive player in front of him. The strong side end blocks the first man in the secondary. This means the first man from the outside in. He does not count the defensive end. In a virtual eight man defensive front it would be the defensive halfback. In a four deep or two and two secondary it would be the cornerback. This is the strong side end's assignment whether he is split or tight.

The slotback blocks the second man from the outside in the secondary. In three deep coverage it would be the safety, while in four deep he would block the strong safety. This assignment stays the same when the slotback is flanked.

The Belly Option Toward the 100 Formation

The belly option is called Right 34 option and Left 33 option. The option refers to the quarterback in relation to keeping the football or pitching to the tailback. The belly option is predetermined as far as the fullback is concerned. In the belly option the quarterback rides the fullback but never hands the football to him. The plays R34 and R33, which were discussed in the last chapter, are the first sequence of the belly option. Figure 5.2 shows the blocking for R134 option against a 5-4 defense.

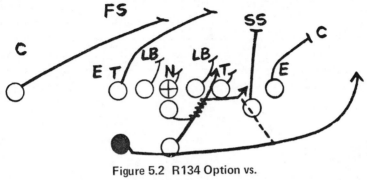

Figure 5.2 R134 Option vs.
5-4 Defense

You might refer to Figure 5.1 to see that all of the blocking rules have been followed in R134 option. Figure 5.3 shows the 34 option from the 100 flex formation.

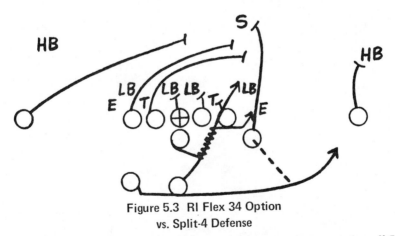

Figure 5.3 Rl Flex 34 Option
vs. Split-4 Defense

The slotback has the rule "second man in the secondary." In Figure 5.3 this would be the safety. However, he will run through the linebacker that is in front of him. If the linebacker is able to search the fullback and then make the play on the quarterback, a coaching point may call for the slotback to block him. With good execution from the backs this linebacker should tie himself up with the fullback.

The Belly Option from 200 Formation

The 200 formation is the pro set. The belly option blocking rules will not change. Since the slotback is now a flanker, when he blocks the second man in the secondary he has a crack block, which is a favorite blocking advantage. The strong side end also has a good blocking angle on the first man in the secondary. Figure 5.4 shows the belly option to the left side from the pro set.

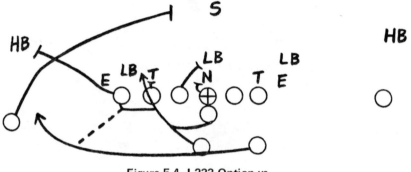

Figure 5.4 L233 Option vs.
5-3 Defense

If a linebacker or a defensive tackle just inside the strong end is causing problems, the strong end will block this defensive player and the flanker will switch to the first man in the secondary. Figure 5.5 shows this blocking adjustment against a 4-3 pro defense.

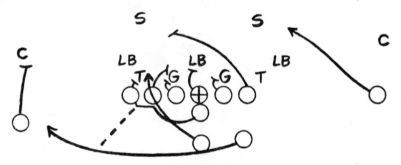

Figure 5.5 L233 Option vs 4-3 Pro

The strong end and flanker will block according to the learned assignment unless the coaching point for the change is sent into the ball game. With experience the strong end and flanker will learn to recognize the various defensive alignments and make the necessary adjustments by themselves.

All members of the offense should be able to diagram some of the common defenses they will face. This will create an awareness of the overall blocking situations and provide them with confidence when carrying out their individual assignments.

The Belly Option Toward the 300 Formation

The blocking assignments are the same. The slotback and strong end merely execute their blocks from a different alignment. Figures 5.6 and 5.7 show the belly option from the 300 formation against a common odd and even defense.

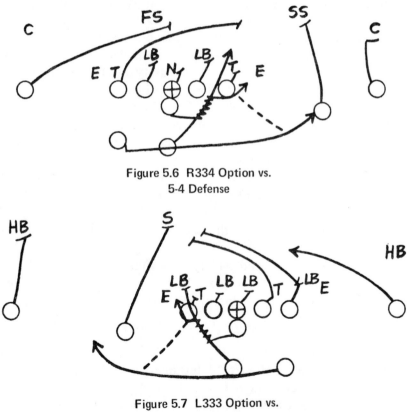

Figure 5.6 R334 Option vs.
5-4 Defense

Figure 5.7 L333 Option vs.
Split-4 Defense

The belly option is not run toward the 400 (power I) formation. It can be run away from the formation, which is a weak side play and will be discussed in the chapter.

The Belly Option Blocking Techniques for the Slotback and the Strong Side End

When the slotback's alignment is the 100 formation he will run through the man in front of him, if there is one, or block this man if a coaching point is called for. He will block the second man in the secondary by being under control enough to make solid contact. A shield or butt block maintaining outside leverage is an adequate block. The slotback can anticipate two moves of this second man in the secondary. If the quarterback keeps the football, this safety will come up quickly. In this case the slotback should dip his tail and come under complete control, then fire into the safety going after the bulk of the safety's body with the head of the slotback to the outside.

If the safety is leveling to the outside the slotback will assume the pitch has been made. In this case he will take the shortest line of interception with the safety and make contact by a driving shoulder block as quickly as possible.

When the slotback is flanked he will crack the second man in the secondary. He must be prepared for three maneuvers of the second man: coming up to make the play on the quarterback, leveling outside to contain the pitch, and dropping back and to the outside to cover outside third. Once the slotback/flanker is close enough for the block on the second man, he can wait for this man to make the move that would indicate where the football is. The slotback will then screen the safety or body block him to the ground.

The strong side end will read the man he is to block in a similar manner. He will block the first man in the secondary unless a coaching point will have him block a man in front of him.

The Backfield Execution for the Belly Option

The fullback must read the four hole in 34 option and the three hole in 33 option to determine his path into the line of scrimmage. If there is no defensive lineman in the hole prior to the snap, the fullback will drive into this hole with the proper fake to force a defensive tackle or linebacker (or both) to make a play on him. The fullback will make the customary pocket for a hand-off by having the inside elbow up. When the quarterback places the football in the fullback's belly the fullback will have very light contact with the ball. Under no circumstances will he tighten down on the football. When the football is removed the fullback will grasp each elbow with the opposite hand and continue into the line. If the fullback is not tackled he should block color that is coming toward the point of attack.

The quarterback will have to read the hole in the same manner the fullback did to place himself in the proper position to ride the fullback. If a defensive lineman is aligned in the hole the quarterback will have to make a slightly larger approach step to the fullback.

The quarterback will reverse out for the belly option. He will pivot on the strong side foot until he can set his weak side foot at a four o'clock position, with this foot pointed slightly toward the top of backfield. He now brings the strong side foot around and steps with this foot to a position where he will meet the fullback. As he brings the strong side around the quarterback extends the football toward the fullback and rides the fullback into the line. To get the maximum ride the quarterback will step into the line with the foot nearest the line of scrimmage and follow up with a step with the back foot. The quarterback will remove the football from the fullback and should be looking directly at the defensive end and approximately one yard in the backfield. The quarterback will proceed down the line, optioning the defensive end. If the quarterback keeps the football he will turn downfield. If he pitches he will execute the pitch by extending the palm of the hand nearest the top of the backfield and float the football into the chest of the tailback, who is four yards outside him and four yards into the backfield.

The tailback opens to the strong side with his strong foot toward the top of the backfield and parallel to the line of scrimmage. This should place him four yards from the line of scrimmage. He should now bow his path toward the corner. If the pitch is to him he should not break stride unless the pitch is poor.

The quarterback should ride the fullback as long as possible for two reasons. A long ride will hold defensive people and will also permit the tailback time to get a "four and four" position for the pitch. Figure 5.8 shows the quarterback, fullback, and tailback footwork for the belly option.

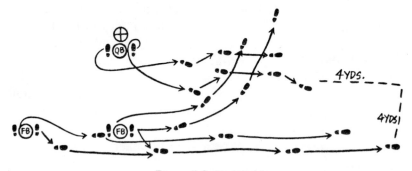

**Figure 5.8 Backfield
Footwork for R34 Option**

The Lead Option Toward the Formation

The other option to the strong side is the lead option to the fullback. The only natural formation the lead option can be used in as a strong side play is the 400 formation. This formation uses the powerback as the lead. In other formations tailback motion has to be used, but can be used very effectively.

The blocking assignments for the strong side lead option are rule blocks for all members of the offense except the slotback, strong side end, and whoever the lead blocker is going to be, which is determined by the formation.

The blocks of the slotback and strong end are determined by which of them because of his alignment is on the outside. The inside blocker of the two will seal the nearest linebacker. The outside blocker will block the second man in the secondary. In 100 formation the slotback will seal the linebacker and the end will block the second man, who will be a safety. In 200 formation the slot, who is now a flanker, is the outside man and therefore will block the second man in the secondary. The strong end seals the linebacker. The lead blocker, either the powerback or the tailback in motion, will block the first man in the secondary. If there is only one blocker outside the offensive tackle he will seal the linebacker instead of blocking the second man in the secondary. Such is the case of the split end in the 400 formation.

The lead option toward the formation is called R18 option and L17 option. The lead option is usually a weak side play. To utilize the lead option as a strong side play the tailback has to be in motion in 100, 200, and 300 formations. If not, the defense will have two people on the outside of the quarterback. One of these people will play the quarterback and the other will take the pitch. By using motion we have a one-on-one situation to that side. Figure 5.9 shows the lead option toward the 100 formation. When motion is used it is inserted between the formation number and the play number that is called in the huddle. If the #4 back is to go in motion toward the formation it is called "40 strong." If he is to go in motion to the weak side it is called "40 weak." The other motions are "20 strong" and "20 weak." The fullback never uses motion. Timing is necessary to get the #4 or #2 backs in particular position at the snap. The backs are instructed to start their motion on the first call of the audibles from the quarterback. This is to make sure the play is not changed at the line. The back in motion has to regulate his speed to be at a certain place at the snap. Practice is certainly necessary for this.

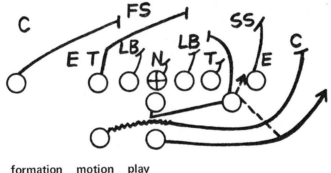

formation   motion   play
Fig. 5.9   (R1)   (40 Strong)   (18 Option) vs. 5-4

The formation, motion, and play are called independently in the huddle. For example, the quarterback would call the play that is shown in Figure 5.9 as "Right one . . . forty strong . . . eighteen option." His snap count would then follow.

In Figure 5.9 excellent blocking angles are shown. No doubt the defense will do something to compensate for the motion. Most four deep secondaries would rotate to the side of the motion. Three deep secondaries will probably adjust linebacker. These are things a scouting report will indicate. It may be necessary to wait until early in the game to find how the opponent will adjust to the motion. Figure 5.10 shows the strong side lead option from the 100 flex formation.

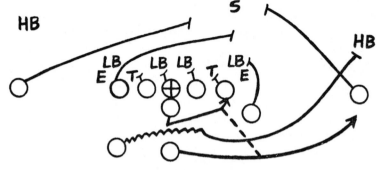

Figure 5.10 (R1 Flex) (40 Strong) (18 Option)
vs. Split-4 Defense

Attacking the defense that rotates, inverts, reverts linebackers, shifts linemen, etc., when motion is used, will be discussed in a later chapter. Figure 5.11 shows the strong side lead option from the pro alignment, and Figure 5.12 shows the lead from the wide slot formation.

Motion toward the formation gives the extra blocker, but if the defense overadjusts the motion may not be effective. Some occasions may call for motion to the weak side by either the tailback or slotback and still run the strong side lead. This of course depends on how the defense adjusts to motion.

As mentioned previously the lead option, without motion, is generally run to the weak side. In this way the tailback can serve as the lead blocker without being in motion. The only formation in which the lead option can be used as a strong side play is the 400 formation. The powerback is the lead in this formation. The use of motion in the 400 formation is not necessary to gain the lead blocker, but perhaps it would be effective to send the tailback in weak motion. The defense would adjust to the weak side, which might weaken their defense to the lead option toward the strong side.

In Figure 5.13 the split end sealed the linebacker because he is the only outside blocker as mentioned earlier in the blocking assignments for 17 and 18 option.

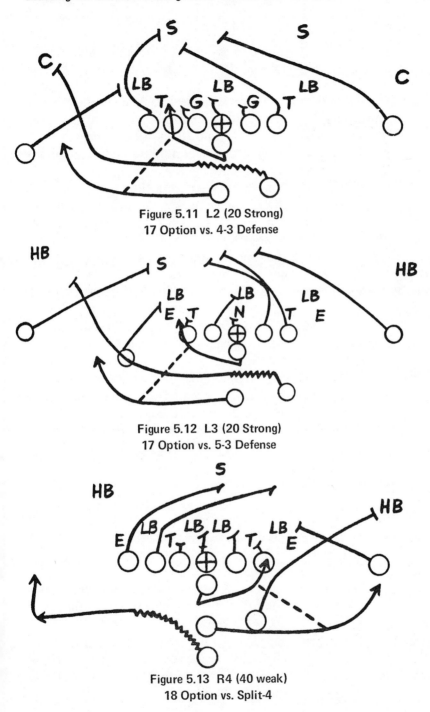

Figure 5.11 L2 (20 Strong)
17 Option vs. 4-3 Defense

Figure 5.12 L3 (20 Strong)
17 Option vs. 5-3 Defense

Figure 5.13 R4 (40 weak)
18 Option vs. Split-4

The Backfield Action of 18 and 17 Lead Options

Considerable time should be spent with the fullbacks to make sure they take no false steps on their take-off. If they do or if they slow considerably when they are tired, they will not be the necessary "four and four" with the quarterback when the pitch is made. The fullback opens to the formation and executes a drop step to the top of the backfield to gain an additional one-half yard in depth. His path is parallel to the line until he receives the pitch. The fullback will cut off of the block by the lead blocker.

To give the fullback time to be in front, the quarterback will receive the snap and back out one step. He will then open to the strong side facing the defensive end. He will keep or pitch when he gets to the outside leg of the strong tackle. The pitch is made with the palm of the hand extending toward the target as he steps with the strong side foot. The first step by the quarterback is made with the weak side foot. He simply drops the foot about eighteen inches straight back and hesitates one-half count. This is followed with a short step with the strong side foot pointed directly at the defensive end.

The tailback would be too far in front of the fullback if he were to take off quickly at the snap. Instead of some false motion in the backfield the tailback is instructed to run under control and then get a good solid piece of the outside man in the secondary. The path of the tailback is toward the line of scrimmage slightly behind the defensive end and then toward the cornerback or whoever forces the play.

The Strong Side Quick Pitch

The strong side quick pitch is run only from the 400 formation, since this is the only formation that has a set back behind the strong tackle. The play is called Right 28 and Left 47. The quick pitch is a weak side play for formations other than the 400. Figure 5.14 gives the blocking rules for the quick pitch.

The assignments from the strong tackle through the weak side are base rule blocks with the elimination of the gap rule. Defensive linemen who are aligned in the gap cannot cut off the quick pitch in the backfield. From an over position they might move down the line and meet the ball carrier. Figure 5.15 shows the quick pitch toward Right 400 formation.

Weak End—Running Lane
Weak Tackle—Cut-Off, Running Lane
Weak Guard—Over, Linebacker
Center—Over, Linebacker Away
Strong Guard—Over, Linebacker, Reach
Strong Tackle—Over, Linebacker
Strong End—Crack the End, Seal Linebacker
Powerback—Ball Carrier
Fullback—Lead
Tailback—Strong Side

**Figure 5.14 Assignments for the
Quick Pitch to the 400 Formations**

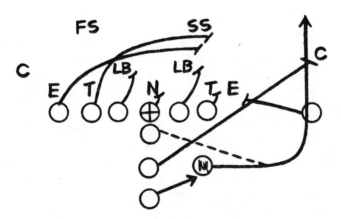

**Figure 5.15 R428 Quick Pitch vs.
5-4 Defense**

The strong end is instructed to crack the defensive end provided he can get a legal blocking surface. If not, he seals the inside. Tailback motion to the weak side would be effective to loosen the cornerback on the split end side. The quick pitch is usually a weak side running play. The backfield action of the quick pitch will be discussed in the next chapter.

Chapter 6

Coaching the Multiple Slot-T Running Game Away from the Formation

The primary objective of the weak side running game is to complement the strong side running game. The weak side attack is highly successful when run into the boundary, especially when your opponent favors the wide side of the field with a monster or some type of rotation.

More than twice we have faced the wide side of the field tendency of our opponent and been very succesful. Our offensive strategy in this situation is to run into the boundary, keeping the football spotted on the near hash line. We are able to communicate with our quarterback easily and, in general, have more offensive organization. It is difficult, at least for a while, for the far side of the field to make adjustments. The weak side attack has been highly successful when our opponent shows an over-shift or employs a slanting defense toward the strong side. The attack has also been very successful against a match-up defense.

One should approach the weak side attack with a great deal of optimism and patience. Anxieties may develop concerning the blocking of the weak side attack due to the sacrifice of the inside blocker created by splitting the end. An even greater concern may be blocking an eagle alignment. The eagle alignment removes some of the blocking advantages the offense might have in another type of defensive alignment. However, you can reach block the eagle alignment when running into the five and seven holes.

Considerable confidence in the quick side attack can be gained when you discover the techniques that have been more effective against the different defense alignments you will face. By forcing your opponent to take notice of the tight slot to your strong side you are able to utilize the weak side attack more effectively. The weak side attack will be discussed and diagrammed from each formation at a time. (See Figure 6.1)

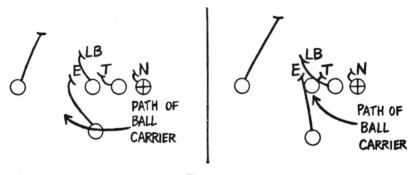

Figure 6.1

THE WEAK SIDE ATTACK FROM 100 FORMATION

The weak side attack will be discussed in the same manner as the strong side attack in relation to attacking the holes. The inside holes are 0, 1, and 3. The outside holes are 5 and 7. For Left formation the inside holes are 0, 2, and 4, with the 6 and 8 holes the outside.

The Counter Trap or the Zero Hole Trap

The only play in the Multiple Slot-T other than a quarterback sneak in which the zero hole is part of the called play is 30 counter. This play is considered part of the weak side attack because the faking action is to the weak side. The blocking for 30 counter is the same as for the two hole trap in Right formation or the one hole trap in Left formation. The weak guard executes the trap. The backfield action involves a fake dive to the tailback, then counter to the fullback. Against an even defense the path of the fullback is in the zero hole or at the tail of the center. Against an odd defense the path of a fullback is more in the hole between the center and the strong guard (in Right formation the two hole, and in Left the one hole). Regardless of the path of the fullback the play number does not change. Figure 6.2 shows the fullback counter from the 100 formation against a 5-4 defense.

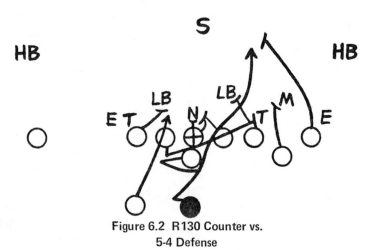

Figure 6.2 R130 Counter vs.
5-4 Defense

The blocking rules for 30 counter are the same as the two hole trap blocking mentioned on p. 49. As mentioned earlier, any dive play is run at the inside hip of the tackle in front of the dive back if the defense is in an even alignment. The dive is practically over guard when attacking an odd defense. This allows the quarterback to make the two-step dive fake in an even and a one-step fake in an odd, then counter to the fullback who is going through the zero hole against an even defense and the two hole against an odd defense. The tailback, fullback, and quarterback determine their footwork when the quarterback gives the odd or even defensive call in the signals.

In an even defense the quarterback steps down the line with a medium step with the weak side foot. This is followed by a fairly large step with the strong side foot. The fake is made to the dive back as the strong side foot is placed on the ground. The weak side foot then becomes the pivot foot. The quarterback turns 180 degrees toward the top of backfield, brings the strong side foot even with the weak side foot, and executes the hand-off to the fullback.

The fullback takes a short step to the weak side with the weak side foot, then toward the line of scrimmage. He receives the hand-off with his weak arm on top as he goes into the zero hole.

Against an odd defense the quarterback takes one less step with the weak side foot and adds this step to his strong side movement to be at the two hole to execute the hand-off to the fullback. The quarterback makes a short step to the weak side with the weak side foot. He then brings his strong foot even with the weak foot as he makes the dive fake. The next movement is to pivot on the strong foot 180 degrees by turning toward the top of the backfield. He takes a medium step toward the strong side with the weak foot, followed by one step with the strong foot to execute the hand-off.

The fullback takes the same step to the weak side but instead of squaring with the line of scrimmage he turns toward the hole between the center and the strong guard. The fullback's actions are deliberate and he should not rush the counter step. The tailback in either case executes a good dive fake by grasping his elbows with the opposite hands after the fake. The closer the dive back and the quarterback without a collision, the less daylight and the greater the deception.

The trapping guard has a short pull. He should find the man he is to trap as soon as he turns his head to the inside. Figure 6.3 shows the fullback counter against an even defense.

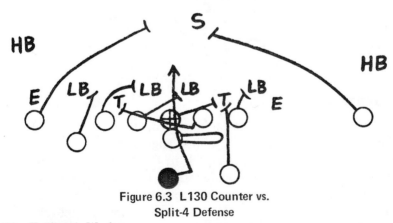

Figure 6.3 L130 Counter vs.
Split-4 Defense

The Fullback Wedge

The fullback wedge is straight ahead and usually a short yardage play. The line blocking is base with the center blocking over, gap away, and linebacker away. The guards block gap, over, linebacker, and the tackles block gap, over, and linebacker. The ends and the slotback block inside to the running lane. A coaching point might allow the center to double-team with the weak guard in an even defensive alignment if there is no linebacker in front of him. A stack in the one hole would usually call for an audible.

The quarterback opens to the weak side and steps back to clear for the fullback as he executes the hand-off. He then carries out a fake to the tailback through the hole between the strong guard and the strong tackle. The fullback receives the hand-off soon enough to slip inside or outside if daylight is there. However, in a less-than-one situation he will hit quick and straight ahead into the one hole or two hole, depending on the formation. The linemen are certainly going to fire off the line to contact the defensive people as soon as possible. Figure 6.4 shows the fullback wedge, which is numbered R31 and L32.

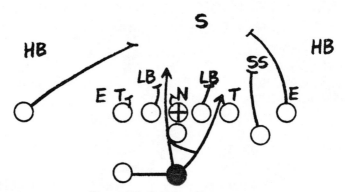

Figure 6.4 R131 vs. 5-4 Defense

The Inside Dive to the Tailback

The inside dive to the tailback, which is R41 and L22, is a good play selection against a split-4 alignment. Unlike a regular dive play where the tailback's path to the hole is determined by the odd or even defensive alignment, the inside dive route will not be altered. If the hole is stacked up an audible will be used. The primary purpose of this play is to hit into the inside linebackers to see if the defense is able to close the middle. If our center and strong guard can come off the ball quickly, with the tailback hitting in the hole quickly, the yardage gained is worthwhile.

The quarterback will open toward the weak side and step

into the backfield and slightly toward the tailback with his lead foot (left foot if moving left, vice-versa). This is followed with a drop step with his inside foot to clear himself from the path of the ball carrier. The football is extended to prevent any body contact. The give is a standard dive hand-off. As the give is made the quarterback will make a short step with the lead foot to widen his stance a little and maintain good balance. The fullback moves behind the tailback and toward the five hole if in Right formation or the six hole if in Left formation.

The blocking in the line is base rule blocks. The center blocks over, gap away, and linebacker away. The guards block gap, over, and linebacker, and the tackles block gap, over, and linebacker. In Figure 6.5 the weak side tackle has to reach the tackle inside him, which is a difficult block if the anchor tackle is closing fast. If the weak tackle blocked the linebacker and let the weak guard block the defensive tackle, the blocks of the center, strong guard, and the strong tackle would move down one man and create the same situation with the other anchor tackle. If the weak tackle can prevent the anchor tackle from penetrating and the tailback hits quickly, the play can be successful blocking the base rules. The ends and slotback block the running lane. Figure 6.5 shows the inside dive against the Split-4 Defense.

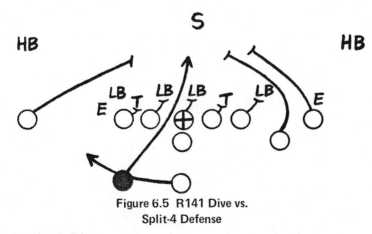

**Figure 6.5 R141 Dive vs.
Split-4 Defense**

The Tailback Dive

The tailback dive play, which is Right 43 and Left 24, is very basic but essential in any offense. Base rule blocking by the linemen is used with the deviation by the ball carrier that was mentioned earlier. When the quarterback calls the defense alignment (odd or even) the tailback knows his route to the hole. The dive is run practically over the weak guard in an odd defense and virtually at the weak tackle in a standard even defense. When the path of the dive back is inside, plays 43 and 41 are similar except that 41 is more to the inside. A dive is difficult to run against a split-4 alignment unless the linebacker near the hole is in a "walk-away" position. If the linebacker has loosened considerably, which he might do on the split end side, the weak tackle may be able to clear the area in front of him, allowing the dive back to hit inside the defensive end. Figure 6.6 shows how the dive would be run against the split-4 defense with a walk-away linebacker.

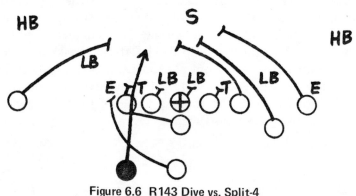

Figure 6.6 R143 Dive vs. Split-4
Defense with a Walk-Away Linebacker

The blocking rules for the linemen are base 4 or 3 hole blocks. The guards have a gap, over, linebacker, and fold rule, but must ignore the fold rule when a dive is called. The tackles block gap, over, and linebacker, and the center blocks over, gap away, and linebacker away. The slotback and the ends block running lane. The fullback moves behind the tailback to the weak side and turns downfield to block. Figure 6.7 shows how the dive is run against an odd defense.

If the defense is an odd alignment the quarterback opens to the weak side with one short step with the weak side foot, then squares up with his strong foot parallel to the weak foot and

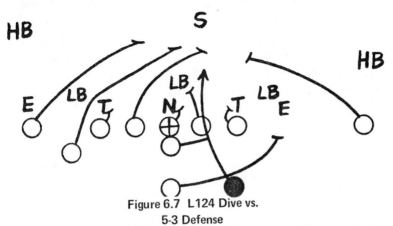

Figure 6.7 L124 Dive vs.
5-3 Defense

executes the hand-off. If the defense is an even, the quarterback will open with the short weak-side foot step and then follow with a sizeable step with the strong foot to place him in position to make the hand-off.

The Fullback Over the Weak Tackle Play

The fullback over the weak side tackle is called R33 and L34. The linemen use their base rule blocks, which will include the fold block for the guard when the defensive alignment calls for it.

When executing R33 and L34, the quarterback spins and gives the fullback approximately two yards behind the line of scrimmage. This enables the fullback to have the run-for-daylight option. The footwork for the quarterback spin is identical to the strong side belly (R34 and L33) that was discussed in Chapter 4. The spin versus the open-out by the quarterback may freeze the linebacker on that side for an instant, allowing the guard or tackle to get to him, which may be all that is needed for the big gain. The spin will also prevent the quarterback from being distracted by a penetrating defense, which could result in a poor hand-off. With the spin he sees no one but the fullback until after the hand-off is made.

The tailback will block the end to the outside. The split end blocks running lane, which will probably be the near halfback. When the guard folds he is instructed to keep tight and turn into the hole, and block the color that shows. This will probably be a linebacker. If the defensive end is playing too tight the guard will block the end outside, and the tailback can lead into the hole. There is a bootleg play off the action of R33 and L34 which will be discussed later. Figure 6.8 shows how R133 is run against a 5-4 defense. Figure 6.9 shows the play against a 5-4 defense with an eagle alignment on the weak side.

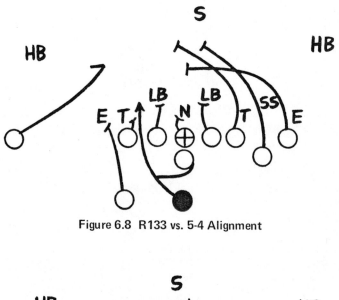

Figure 6.8 R133 vs. 5-4 Alignment

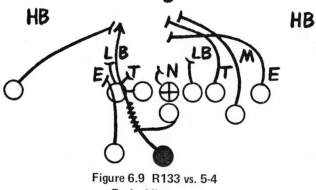

Figure 6.9 R133 vs. 5-4
Eagle Alignment

In a split-4 alignment the weak tackle blocks gap and the weak guard folds. If the linebacker in front of the weak guard fires this could create a problem, but most of the time the split-4 technique is to close the anchor tackles and scrape off for the linebackers. When the fold rule is executed it allows the weak guard to seal off the inside linebacker by blocking the outside linebacker and walling off the inside linebacker. The fullback cuts outside if he is able to. Figure 6.10 shows L134 against a split-4 alignment.

Figure 6.11 shows the footwork for R33. L34 would be the opposite.

The quarterback pivots on his weak side foot as he swings the strong foot around where he can step toward the fullback. He is nearly parallel to but approximately two yards from the line of scrimmage. A step is then made with the weak foot to enable the quarterback to square up with the fullback. The quarterback will ride for an instant by reaching back for the fullback, but with no intention of keeping the football. The quarterback will finish by faking a bootleg wide.

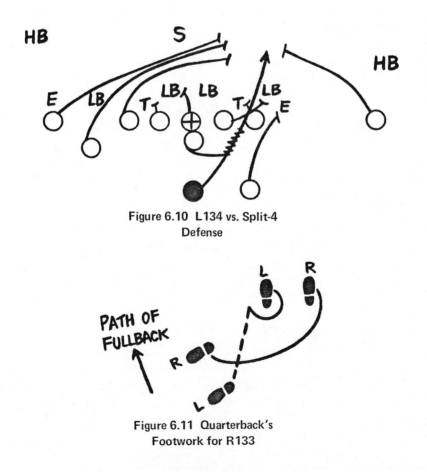

Figure 6.10 L134 vs. Split-4
Defense

Figure 6.11 Quarterback's
Footwork for R133

The Outside Trap to the Weak Side

The outside trap to the weak side is called R25 trap and L46 trap. It can actually be either an inside trap or an outside trap, depending on the alignment of the defensive tackle. If the defensive tackle's alignment places him head-up or outside the weak tackle, he is the man to be trapped. If his alignment is inside the weak tackle, the man to be trapped is the defensive end. The weak side tackle and the tailback have to read the alignment of the defensive tackle to apply their trap blocking assignments. Figure 6.12 gives the blocking assignments for the outside trap.

Weak End—Near Halfback
Weak Tackle—Inside, Linebacker
Weak Guard—Over, Gap, Linebacker, Outside
Center—Over, Gap Away, Linebacker Away
Strong Guard—Pull block first to show
Strong Tackle—Over, Linebacker, Running Lane
Strong End—Running Lane
Tailback—If tackle is inside, block Linebacker
        If tackle is over or outside, block End

**Figure 6.12 Blocking Rules for
the Outside Trap**

Figures 6.13 and 6.14 show how the trap blocking rules hold up against a 5-4 with an eagle alignment on the weak side, and against a 6-2 Defense.

The outside trap to the weak side is off the action of the strong side belly. In Right formation the quarterback spins and makes the 34 fake, then hands to the slotback who is nearly parallel and within three yards of the line of scrimmage. The fake is made by placing the football in front of the fullback and removing it by bringing the elbows into the sides, then a slight pivot on the balls of both feet to make the outside hand-off to the slotback. The slot takes the football by using the dive hand-off technique.

The slotback will pick up the pulling guard, who is two to three yards in front of him. He will make his cut downfield off the block of the pulling guard. The slotback must be under control enough to make the early cut if the defensive tackle is aligned over or outside the weak tackle, and also have the momentum to get to

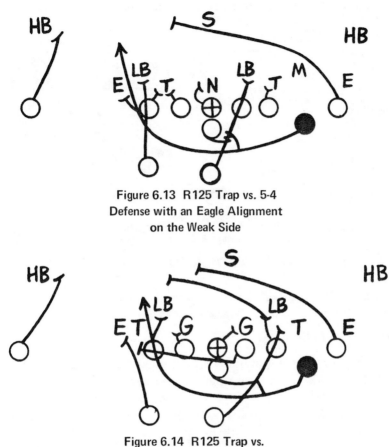

Figure 6.13 R125 Trap vs. 5-4
Defense with an Eagle Alignment
on the Weak Side

Figure 6.14 R125 Trap vs.
6-2 Defense

the outside. The slotback looks for the inside route first, but if he doesn't have it continues to the outside.

The tailback will take a quick counter step to the inside for deception, then back to pick up his block. The fullback after his fake into the four hole must continue into the line to fill for the pulling guard.

The action of the trap would be more deceptive if the tailback were to sprint toward the strong side as he does on the belly option, but if the tailback is used as a blocker we won't have to guess whether or not a linebacker will take the fake or if a defensive end might close and make it difficult for us to trap him.

Figure 6.15 shows the footwork of the quarterback and the slotback for the outside trap in Right formation.

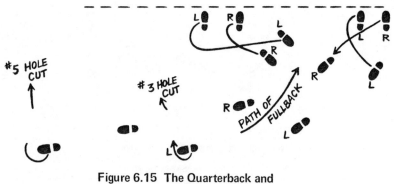

#5 HOLE CUT

#3 HOLE CUT

PATH OF FULLBACK

**Figure 6.15 The Quarterback and
Slotback Footwork for R125 Trap**

THE OUTSIDE ATTACK TO THE WEAK SIDE

The outside attack to the weak side includes two bootlegs, a lead option, a quick-pitch, and a reverse.

The Weak Side Bootlegs

The bootlegs are actually in a special play category and are used to attack a defense that is jammed inside and to take advantage of the quarterback who has exceptional speed. The bootlegs are run off the dive and the fullback over tackle plays. Since the numbers of the dives are 43 and 24 the bootlegs are communicated by merely inserting the word "bootleg" after the call. The same thing is true for the fullback over tackle which, for the bootlegs, would be 34 bootleg and 33 bootleg. This communicates to all members of the offense that a dive fake or a fullback over tackle fake will be made, but the quarterback will keep the football. The linemen should execute their three or four hole blocks and not release too quickly. Figure 6.16 shows R143 bootleg against a 5-4 defense.

Most defensive ends, expecially those on the split-end side (unless the defensive end is in a walk-away or similar alignment), are virtually on top of the dive play and have a natural reaction to the inside hand-off. This enables the quarterback, with a good dive fake, to get outside the defensive end. After the quarterback makes the dive fake, he steps around the collision of the dive and

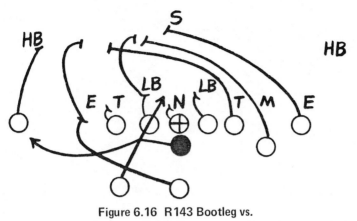

Figure 6.16 R143 Bootleg vs.
5-4 Defense

the tackler, then sprints to the boundary with the football on the
outside hip. The fullback, whose action on the dive is to slant,
hooks the end or continues as a lead blocker, depending on
whether or not the defensive end has been beaten.

The weak guard blocks base rule but tries to obtain outside
leverage when the block is the linebacker. The guard does not fold
on the dive or the dive bootleg. He doesn't have time. The weak
tackle blocks base rule with outside leverage on the over block.
The split end pushes the near halfback deep. The quarterback
wants to keep his feet moving when making the dive fake to
enable him to reach full speed as soon as possible.

The 43 and 24 bootlegs are more effective when the dive is
run at the weak tackle (the situation of an even defense). The
reason for this is because the fake is made nearer to the defensive
end, allowing the quarterback to be nearer to the outside running
room when the fake is made. Figure 6.17 shows the dive bootleg
against an even defense.

The fullback bootleg is called R33 and L34. The linemen
block base rule with the outside leverage objective. The tailback
now hooks the end. This bootleg is more effective when the
defensive tackle is inside the weak tackle. Figure 6.18 shows L134
bootleg against an eagle alignment on the weak side.

The split end pushes the near halfback deep or blocks him.
The linemen block base. The fullback must carry out a good fake
to prevent the linebacker on that side from releasing to the
outside. The weak guard will usually block that linebacker, but the

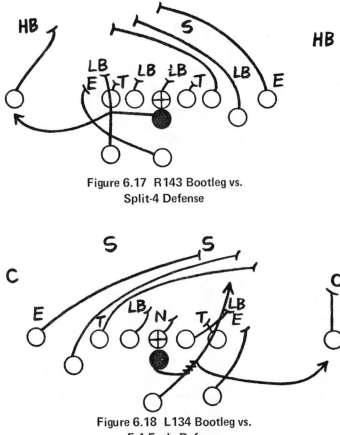

Figure 6.17 R143 Bootleg vs.
Split-4 Defense

Figure 6.18 L134 Bootleg vs.
5-4 Eagle Defense

fullback can help. The weak guard does fold when the situation calls for it.

The quarterback will spin with the same footwork as play 33 and 34, which is the belly option. The quarterback will ride the fullback, bring the football out of the fullback's stomach, and bootleg toward the boundary by placing the ball on his far hip.

The Weak Side Lead Option

The weak side lead option is called Right 17 and Left 18. These options open several possibilities in the weak side attack. With good execution the lead option can be a consistent gainer. The action also opens several passing lanes, which will be discussed later.

The blocks of the center through the strong side end are base blocks. The strong tackle, slotback, and strong end can release to the running lane. The weak guard will block the base rule, but when the linebacker rule applies the guard can prevent penetration by this linebacker and then go to the running lane. The weak guard cannot very well obtain an outside position on this linebacker, and in most cases this will be the linebacker the split end will seal. The most critical block at the line of scrimmage is that of the weak tackle. He must prevent the defensive tackle from penetrating, which is difficult when he has to reach block. The reach block may prevent the defensive tackle from penetrating but, because of his outside alignment on the weak tackle, he may be able to make the play on the quarterback if the pitch is not made. This would place two defensive people outside the quarterback, one to play the quarterback and the other to contain the pitch man. This is certainly an undersirable match-up when executing an option.

Another vital block is that of the split end. He will seal the linebacker nearest him. The end has a very desirable angle and should be able to make this block with frequent success. The normal alignment of the split end is seven yards outside the weak tackle, but for the lead option he will cut this split to five yards to be in a position to seal without allowing the linebacker to get upfield. The tailback is the lead blocker. He will dip toward the line of scrimmage slightly, to prevent his block from being early, then block the first man from the outside in the secondary.

The first action of the quarterback is to take one drop step toward the top of the backfield with his strong foot, which is still pointed at 12 o'clock. He will then open to the weak side and take the next step with his weak foot, pointed directly where a defensive end would normally be aligned. This allows the quarterback to challenge the defensive end from a slight angle that would give him more drive if he did not make the pitch. A greater advantage of the drop step is to allow the fullback an extra step to be in a "four and four" position for the pitch. The fullback must have at least average speed for the lead option. The quarterback drives to the outside leg of the weak tackle before he options. When the quarterback executes the pitch he will give the defensive end his inside shoulder and execute the pitch from the palm of the hand as described earlier. The pitch is made to the chest level of the fullback. Figures 6.19 and 6.20 show the R17 and L18 options against three common defenses.

Against a 4-3 defense the weak tackle will not attempt to reach the defensive tackle to his outside. This defensive tackle will have to play the quarterback if the split end executes a good block on the outside linebacker. A coaching point would be used that would allow the weak tackle to block against the grain or block the safety. Figure 6.21 shows the lead option against a 5-3 defense.

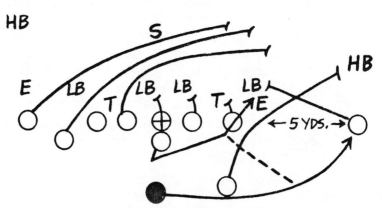

**Figure 6.19 L118 Option vs.
Split-4 Defense**

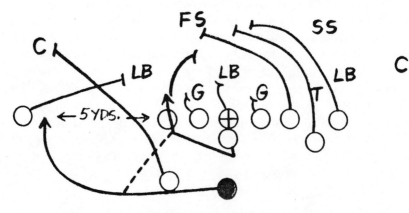

**Figure 6.20 R117 Option vs.
4-3 Pro Defense**

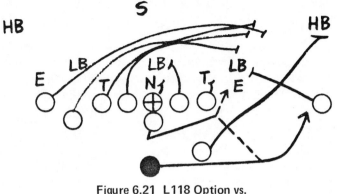

Figure 6.21 L118 Option vs.
5-3 Defense

The Weak Side Quick-Pitch

The weak side quick-pitch is call Right 47 and Left 28. The tailback and fullback must move quickly on the snap. The tailback takes a step away from the line of scrimmage to allow the fullback to gain. The tailback then sprints toward the boundary with a slightly bowed path, again to allow the fullback to gain a leading position. The tailback will receive the pitch on his first or second outside step; therefore he is looking toward the quarterback as soon as he raises from the snap. The fullback will run a slant line to become the lead. The quarterback makes the pitch, without hesitation, as soon as he receives the snap from the center. He will step directly toward the target area, which is the tailback's chest, with his weak side foot. This step is elongated and is made simultaneously with the pitch. The pitch is an underhanded effort that is made with both hands, guided more by the weak hand and powered more by the strong hand. The hands are rotated to the back third of the football and underneath, with the thumbs cradling the ball at about the side seams. This type of pitch has been found to be very reliable and effective.   *162857*

The center blocks base rule. The weak guard blocks inside to prevent the penetration of a lineman who might interfere with the pitch. His second rule is to block linebacker or release, to fan block, at the running lane. We are not concerned with blocking any down linemen from the nose of the weak guard to the nose of the weak tackle. This lineman cannot get to the quarterback, the tailback, or interfere with the pitch. The weak tackle blocks reach or linebacker. The split end, with a minimum split of five yards, cracks the defensive end. The first thought of the split end is to assume the defensive end is going to smash. The split end will angle down and gain backfield depth. If the defensive end does smash he can go after him immediately. If the defensive end does not smash, the split end can come under control and wait for the defensive end to make the play on the pitch man. The split end should not block any lower than thigh level and should put the defensive end on the ground. The split end will have to wait for the defensive end to turn to have a legal blocking surface. The block is usually a blind side block as far as the defensive end is concerned, since most defensive ends will have to turn to the outside to make the play on the tailback. If the defensive end does not turn the split end will turn downfield to pick up the pursuit. Figures 6.22 and 6.23 show the weak side quick pitch against a 5-4 and a 5-4 Eagle Alignment.

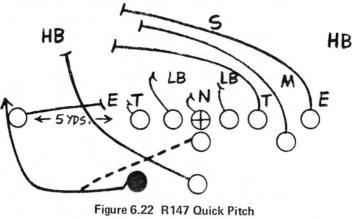

Figure 6.22 R147 Quick Pitch
vs. 5-4 Defense

The Weak Side Reverse

The weak side reverse is R127 and L148, and is run from the action of the strong side power sweep. Certainly the success of the sweep will determine the surprise factor of the reverse. The reverse, though used sparingly, has been a highly effective play in the Multiple Slot-T Attack. The determining factor is surprise, since there are few blocking advantages. Another factor to the

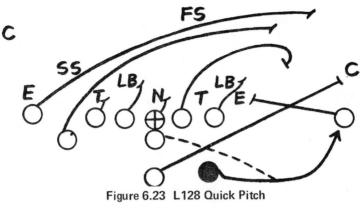

**Figure 6.23 L128 Quick Pitch
vs. 5-4 Eagle Defense**

success of the reverse is to make the sweep look real. If the defensive end on the weak side can be blocked, the yardage gained will be sizeable. When the power sweep in Chapter 4 was discussed it was mentioned then that the quarterback would move toward the weak side after the pitch to the tailback. One of the reasons for this is for the quarterback to block the weak side defensive end on the reverse. The split end pushes the near halfback deep to give the slotback running room when he clears the defensive end.

The center, weak guard, and weak tackle reach and wall to the inside. The strong side linemen block initially as they would on the power sweep, then release to the running lane.

The quarterback makes the power sweep pitch, then moves to the weak side to hook the end. The fullback does not have to follow through with his block since the action has gone the other way before he reaches the defensive end. The tailback receives the pitch and keeps the ball in his hands because the hand-off is made to the slotback almost immediately. The hand-off is outside using the dive technique. The slotback gains depth with his first step, which is taken with the inside foot. He reaches sprint speed still veering slightly toward the top of the backfield. The slotback receives the hand-off with the near arm up. The exchange should be made at about the zero hole. The path of the ball carrier should provide the proper angle to clear the defensive end. However, if the defensive end is there the ball carrier is instructed to turn inside. He should not attempt to get around the defensive end by gaining more depth. This would usually result in a sizeable loss.

The tailback should receive the football at belt level, which would enable him to keep his palms up and allow a smooth hand-off to the slotback. Figures 6.24 and 6.25 show the reverse against an odd and even defense.

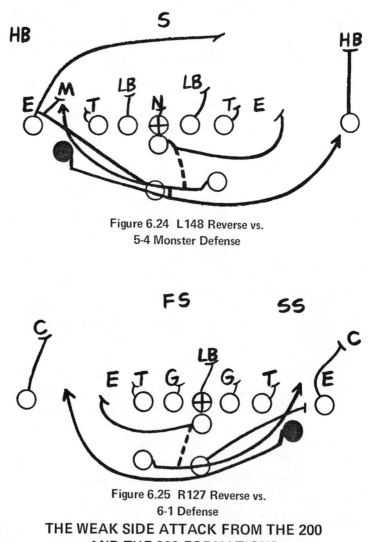

Figure 6.24 L148 Reverse vs.
5-4 Monster Defense

Figure 6.25 R127 Reverse vs.
6-1 Defense

THE WEAK SIDE ATTACK FROM THE 200
AND THE 300 FORMATIONS

Since the only difference between formations 100, 200, and 300 is the alignment of the slotback, the weak side attacks for 200 and 300 formations are virtually the same as that of the 100 formation. The exception to this is when the slotback is the ball carrier, which is the outside trap and the reverse. These two plays and the inside trap are the only three plays that are not used when attacking the weak side in 200 and 300 formations. The Multiple Slot-T does not include any weak side plays for the 200 and 300 formations that the 100 formation does not have. However, in all probability, there will be a different defensive secondary appearance when the 200 and 300 formations are used.

THE WEAK SIDE ATTACK FROM THE 400 FORMATION

The 400 formation, which is the formation from which the shift prior to the snap will occur, is virtually an offense within itself. However, the weak side attack includes only seven plays, with only two of these plays being different from plays of other formations. The 400 formation is the only formation in which the weak side end is not split. The basis for determining Right or Left formation, as mentioned in Chapter 2, is by the alignment of the backs. Actually, if the offense aligned in Right 400 formation, put the second man in the I in weak side motion, and snapped the football when this back was about seven yards outside the weak side end, the formation would be identical to Left 200. By using motion of the backs any formation of the Multiple Slot-T can look like most of the other formations. However, regardless of the formation, with or without motion, the basic rules of blocking and execution do not change. This merely allows the offense to be multiple by showing the defense several things which they must adjust to, but keeps it simple for the offensive player to learn and execute.

Some of the plays called strong side plays when using formations 100, 200, and 300 are actually weak side plays in the 400 formation. The interior linemen learn the plays by the holes, so Right or Left formation means very little to them.

The reason for splitting the end on the side of the formation, where the power back is, is to add pressure to the defense. In formations 100 and 200 the defense is adjusted to the tight end side with either a monster, inverted safety, rotated backfield or something similar. In the 300 formation the defense will adjust to the wide slot. For the 400 formation the defense has to decide whether to adjust to the tight end side or the powerback side. Using motion forces the defense to make still another adjustment, either toward or away from their previous adjustment. In Right 400 formation the weak side attack, which is away from the powerback, is considerably different from the weak side attack for formations 100, 200, and 300. The plays are in the total offense they have simply changed around.

The weak side attack from the 400 formation will be discussed for the two inside holes first, then for the off-tackle and wide holes. The plays will not be any different from any strong side or weak side plays mentioned earlier. Keep in mind the #4 back is the second man in the I in formation Right, while the #2 back is the second man in Left formation. Actually, a diagram will be adequate for most plays of the 400 weak side attack.

The Fullback Wedge

The fullback wedge is 31 and 32 regardless of the formation. All blocking rules are the same as the one and two hole rules mentioned earlier. The only change is that of the alignment and patterns of the backs. Figure 6.26 shows how the fullback wedge would look as a weak side play from the 400 formation. The side of the powerback determines the formation.

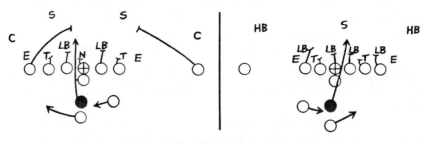

Figure 6.26 R431 and L432

The Weak Side Isolation to the Tailback

There are two isolations to the tailback, who is the second man in the I. They are very similar. The defense determines which is used. One is between the center and the weak guard and is called 41 and 42 isolation. The other is between the weak guard and the weak tackle hole and is called 43 and 44 isolations. The power I with the split end tight (400 tight formation) is used as a short yardage and goalline offense. Figure 6.27 shows the tailback isolation between the center and the weak guard hole.

Figure 6.28 shows the three and the four hole isolations from the 400 formation. On all of the isolations when the tailback is the second man in the I the quarterback merely opens to the side of the play and allows the fullback to clear, then executes the hand-off to the tailback.

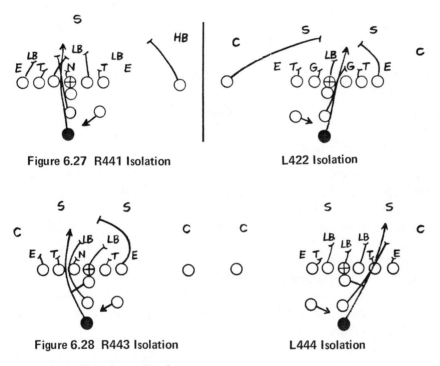

Figure 6.27 R441 Isolation   L422 Isolation

Figure 6.28 R443 Isolation   L444 Isolation

The Weak Side Cross-Buck

The weak side cross-buck is identical to the strong side cross-buck. It is merely run from a different formation, which makes it a weak side play. The play numbers are the same as the strong side, 44X and 23X. (See Figure 6.29)

The Weak Side Belly

The weak side belly is R433 and L434. All blocking assignments are the same. The tailback has to execute his assignment from a different position. Figure 6.30 shows the weak side belly from the 400 formation.

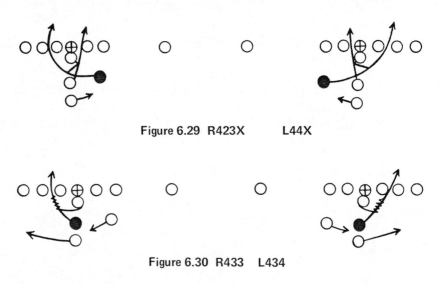

Figure 6.29 R423X   L44X

Figure 6.30 R433   L434

The Weak Side Belly Option

The weak side belly option for the 400 formation requires the second man in the I to execute his block from a different position. His assignment is the second man in the secondary. The end on the side of the play blocks the first man. The fullback runs through the linebacker near the off-tackle hole. If the ride by the quarterback is successful the linebacker will have to play the fullback. A coaching point that was mentioned in Chapter 4 may require the end to block inside and the back to take the first man in the secondary. Figure 6.31 shows the belly option, which is R 433 option and L434 option.

Figure 6.31 R433 Option   L434 Option

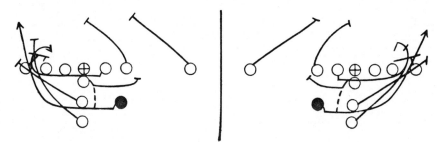

Figure 6.32 R425 Power L446 Power

The Weak Side Power

The final play in the weak side attack from the 400 formation is the power off-tackle. This play can be vey effective if the defense has adjusted considerably to the powerback side. The power play is R425 power and L446 power. The blocking assignments are the same except the weak end double-teams with the tackle or blocks inside rule since the slotback is not there. The second man in the I will lead through the hole and block color. Figure 6.32 shows the power play to each side of the 400 formation.

The strong and weak side plays for the four formations of the Multiple Slot-T, with and without motion, cannot possibly be run in one game. However, a solid game plan using what the coach feels he can attack the defense with is available. It merely means concentrating on a few areas of the offense. The main advantage is that there is not a great deal of new teaching. What the game plan calls for is included in the overall scheme of the offense.

PART 3

Multiple Slot-T Passing Game

**7. Establishing Pass Zones
for the Multiple Slot-T Attack**

**8. Strengthening Types of
Multiple Slot-T Pass Protection**

**9. Organizing Multiple Slot-T
Pass Patterns and Routes**

Chapter 7

Establishing Pass Zones
for the Multiple Slot-T Attack

The wide receiver-quarterback combination is the most effective phase of a pass offense. Each of the formations of the Multiple Slot-T with the exception of the 400 Tight formation has a wide receiver, the split end.

It would be difficult to double-cover the split end in the 100 formation without sacrificing something to the inside. If a linebacker or a defensive end on the weak side attempted to cover the short zone in front of the split end by using a walk-away alignment, the weak guard and weak tackle area would be vulnerable to the run. If the safety covered deep and the cornerback or halfback covered the split end short, the slot side would be vunerable to a pass or a run depending on the alignment of the secondary on the slot side. Of course, if the offense passed only in the obvious passing situations, the defense could effectively adjust to double-cover the split end. The 100 flex formation has both ends as wide receivers, which would make it impossible to draw double coverage to each side.

The 200 formation has a split end and a flanker, which is the usual pro alignment. Most formation strengths would be toward the flanker side since there is a tight end. Both wide receivers being equal, this would often mean the split end would draw single coverage.

The 300 formation, which employs a wide slot, spreads the defense. Passes from this formation concentrate on seam and out routes. The slot and the strong side end could be adjusted to be "twin" receivers.

The 400 formation still has the split end-quarterback combination. Flood and flare routes can be effective from this formation.

THE PASS ZONES

The pass zones of the Multiple Slot-T are established by merely projecting the offensive line openings downfield. The even and the odd numbered passing zones are always the same regardless of Right or Left formation. These zones are the frame of reference from which pass routes are established, but some teminology or description is necessary for the passes as they were for the running plays. The numbering system for the backs is the same for calling pass plays as for the running plays. The number assigned to the ends becomes significant in the pass offense.

The left end is assigned the number seven and the right end is the number eight. The pass zones to the left of the center are one, three, five, and seven. To the right are two, four, six, and eight. The zero is over center but is not used in any of the pass calls. Figure 7.1 shows the passing zones and the number of the receivers. The numbers of the receivers do not change when their alignment changes.

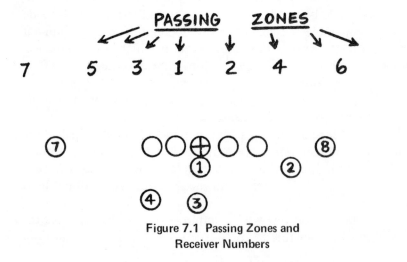

Figure 7.1 Passing Zones and
Receiver Numbers

The zones shown in Figure 7.1 are the basic frame of reference for calling pass plays. The footwork and distance of the receivers are taught as verbal routes. For example, a standard square-out route for the left end is numbered 77. The receiver is taught a square-out route and told it is pass play seventy-seven and he is the primary receiver. The individual teaching of the routes and how the receivers read the coverage of the secondary will be discussed in Chapter 9.

The numbers of the passing plays identify the basic route the back or the end will run. Only the number of the primary receiver is called. This is referred to as a "called" route. The other receivers will learn a companion route or an assignment for the particular called receiver and route. These are referred to as "learned" routes. Since the called route merely places a receiver in a pass zone, some verbalization is necessary to have the particular route that is desired. Some pass plays have the same numbers, but there is not enough repetition to be confusing. For example, as mentioned previously, pass #77 is the left end on a square-out route. The 77 take-off is another route that is run from the square-out. Figure 7.2 shows the numbers of a few basic routes of the Left and the Right Ends.

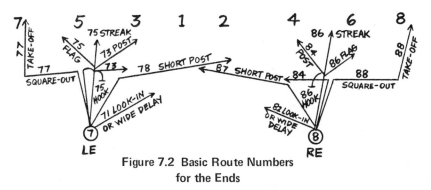

Figure 7.2 Basic Route Numbers
for the Ends

The basic routes are similar to a pass "tree" but are actually determined by the zone the receiver will be in or near when he catches the football.

When the #2 and the #4 backs are a slot, flanker, or a back in long motion, their routes are similar to the ends in relation to the zone number and the route description. The numbers two and four are used with the zone number. Figure 7.3 shows the basic routes of the #2 and the #4 backs when their alignment is outside an offensive tackle.

Figure 7.4 shows the basic routes of the #4 back when he is the tailback, and Figure 7.5 shows the same routes with the #2 back as the tailback.

The only basic route for the fullback is R38 and L37 passes. This is a play action pass in which the fullback runs a flat route. The preceding descriptions will be discussed in detail in Chapter 9, Organizing Multiple Slot-T Pass Patterns and Routes.

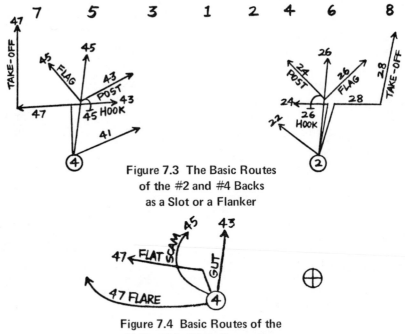

Figure 7.3 The Basic Routes
of the #2 and #4 Backs
as a Slot or a Flanker

Figure 7.4 Basic Routes of the
Tailback in Right Formation

Terminology of Pass Zones

The purpose of discussing the terminology of pass routes is to eliminate misunderstandings in the terminology different coaches use. A "streak" route to some might be a "fly" route to others. The "take-off" is often called a "hitch." The terminology one uses is not important if there is no misunderstanding between coaches and players. The terminology of the route and a brief description

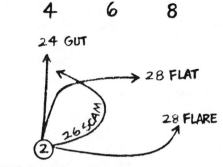

**Figure 7.5 Basic Routes of the
Tailback in Left Formation**

of each will be discussed. The complete route will be discussed in Chapter 9.

The "square-out" in the Multiple Slot-T is a receiver taking a slightly outside route to a point that is usually seven yards from the line of scrimmage. Here he will control his steps and break squarely to the outside. The cut is made from the inside foot. The depth the receiver goes will be determined by the cushion of the defender and the type of coverage the receiver reads. The square-out is run in the seven and the eight zones, depending on the odd or even side. The "take-off" is the square-out and downfield route. The square route is taken but the angle, after the first cut, is not completely square, nor is the cut downfield. The purpose of this is to prevent the loss of momentum.

In the five and six zones are routes that involve the receiver releasing straight downfield. The "streak" route involves a simple sprint from the line of scrimmage. Sometimes a change-of-pace streak is effective. The "flag" route is a seven-yard 45 degree cut to the outside. A slightly outside path should be taken from the line of scrimmage to prevent the loss of momentum. The post route is a seven-yard, slightly inside route, with the 45 degree cut toward the inside.

The "hook" route is a straight release to a seven yard distance. The hook is executed by stopping and pivoting on the inside leg. The outside shoulder turns back toward the line of scrimmage during the pivot. The purpose of this is to produce some confusion for the defender. The square-out route involves planting the inside foot and driving outside by using this leg as leverage. When the foot is planted, the reverse pivot can make the hook effective. The streak, flag, and hook routes are run in the five or six zones, depending on which side is called.

The "trail-in" route is run into the three or four zone. It usually involves a receiver to the inside who is clearing for the intended receiver. Here the receiver takes a slightly outside seven-yard path to draw a defender. He comes under control and drives off the outside leg to trail to the inside. When trailing, he is reading the underneath coverage of the linebackers to get himself in the open.

The basic routes in the one and two zones are a look-in for a wide receiver and a wide delay route for a tight end. On the look-in the receiver takes one downfield step with the outside foot, then drives underneath the secondary at approximately a 25 degree angle. The wide delay for the tight end involves a two-count block on the defensive end, then releasing between the linebackers or underneath them if they have dropped too deep.

For a set back, a "flare" route is a drop step outside and a sprint toward the sidelines. The flare route is also used as a "throw-back" or "back door" pass. The "gut" route is straight through the line of scrimmage and usually a streak deep. The "seam" route is outside the defensive end and a trail back to the five or six zones. This resembles a circle route. The "flat" route releases inside the defensive end. Most defensive ends will allow the inside release of a back. However, they are usually attracted by the back that attempts to release across their face. A screen to a back should be executed by having the back release inside the defensive end unless the end is playing extremely soft.

Advantages of Pass Zones

The pass zones are in an exact area of the field, allowing the pass receiver and the quarterback to know where the ball should be thrown. The number of the pass directs the receiver to an area. The verbal description, after some of the passes, calls for a particular maneuver. Simplicity is achieved by using pass zones.

Required Adjustments

The pass routes that have been mentioned are the way they come from a drawing board. Certainly they must be run with this accuracy most of the time or no timing between the quarterback and the receiver could be attained. The receiver is mainly responsible for the timing of the pass. Under normal circumstances the quarterback will release the football in a set amount of time. The receiver must run his route and be near that zone as the quarterback releases the ball. As the quarterback reads the coverage, if it is not possible to hit the primary receiver, he will look for the secondary receiver. If this isn't possible the quarterback will look for a hole in the line. Receivers should not be over-coached to break a route.

The purpose of using seven yards as the distance for a receiver to make his cut is because much deeper and the quarterback will not have adequate time. Also, unless the quarterback has an exceptionally strong arm the pass might not arrive on time. Seven yards will force the secondary to retreat to maintain the proper cushion.

COACHING POINTS FOR AN EFFECTIVE PASSING ATTACK

For an exceptional passing attack the necessary ingredient is an exceptional passer. However, an effective passing game can be attained with the average passer. Effective passers can be developed.

The Passer

The coach will spend considerable time with the passer. Certainly the passer will show some ability to throw the football, but the coach will have to polish him. The best way to select the quarterback is to get to him early. If the program allows, the coach could select two or three possible candidates at the eighth or ninth grade level, spend some time with them, and then see which one or two of these works out. If this isn't possible, a tenth grader will require considerable attention. The throwing motion, over or under striding, developing the sources of power, and throwing from different positions all require considerable practice. The quarterback will work more hours than any member of the offense. Figure 7.6 shows a warm-up drill that is very effective when practicing setting up, striding, throwing, and changing direction.

The receivers are three yards across the line of scrimmage. The quarterback receives the snap and executes the regular five steps of pocket protection to a depth of seven yards from the line

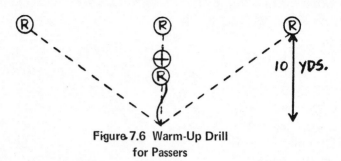

**Figure 7.6 Warm-Up Drill
for Passers**

of scrimmage. He then sets-up, with his feet nearly shoulder width and his left shoulder, if he is right-handed, pointing toward the line of scrimmage. As he draws up to the throwing position the coach gives the command "Right," "Left," or "Middle." The quarterback fires the football to the right, left, or middle receiver, depending on the command. The quarterback has warmed his arm enough to be able to throw the football hard. More than one group can work, but it is difficult for only one coach to see the quarterbacks. This is repeated several times. After a few times the quarterback is alerted the command will change. As the quarterback draws into the throwing motion the coach will shout for one of the receivers, and before the quarterback can release the ball he will change it to another receiver.

For example, the quarterback has drawn into a throwing motion and the coach yells "Right." The quarterback starts into the throwing motion. The coach then changes to "Middle." The quarterback must then check his delivery, return to a throwing position, and fire to the middle receiver. If the passers half-heartedly throw the first command, do not give a second command. If they hear no second command they are to fire the football. Figure 7.7 shows another passing drill for developing distance perception.

After the quarterback is set to throw the coach commands "short," "middle," or "long." The quarterback responds by throwing to the appropriate receiver. After a while the command can be changed to check the pass from a short to a deep or one of the other combinations.

If the quarterback is throwing the football consistently low he is overstriding (setting his foot down before he releases the football). He should be taught to hit the receiver between the

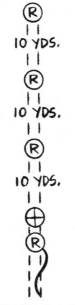

Figure 7.7 Depth Judgment
Passing Drill

eyes. Drills should be developed to have the quarterback throw while running left and right with and without a moving receiver. The same thing is true for running backward and forward. The quarterback will be able to improve his passing skills with drills similar to these. The following tips would be helpful for improving passing skills:

1. When sprinting right with a parallel receiver moving in the same direction it is not necessary to lead the receiver. Merely throw the palm of the passing hand directly at the receiver.

2. When moving left (for a right-handed quarterback) take some power away from the delivery. The back muscles are now being used and the football can actually be thrown farther.

3. When moving toward the receiver take some power away. There is a tendency to overthrow.

4. When backing away from a receiver put more power into the throw.

5. If timing is poor the coach could stand behind the quarterback and shout "Throw" at the appropriate time when the release of the football should be made.

The Receiver

If a boy shows no ability to catch the football and he is older than junior high school, he will probably never be an adequate receiver. He does not possess the hand-eye coordination, proper muscular control, or the mental factors. Significant improvement can be made by the boy who has some talent. Confidence is the key factor. In most cases the football should be caught with the hands. It is preferable to have the thumbs in. Of course the receiver cannot slap at the football. The hands should "give" with the catch, then bring the ball to the chest and under the arm. Concentration should constantly be stressed. A receiver should expect a poorly thrown pass each time. He will make some great catches this way. He should also catch the football at eye level even if he has to break stride to do so. The drill in Figure 7.6 would be helpful to the receiver as well as to the quarterback. A coach would throw at different parts of a receiver's body to get him accustomed to looking for the football and improving his hand-eye coordination. Figure 7.8 is a drill that is useful for the receiver to develop the ability to catch the football with people around.

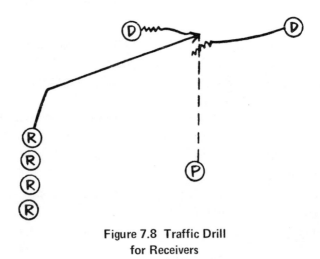

**Figure 7.8 Traffic Drill
for Receivers**

The receiver runs a short post or a similar route. The far defender takes an angle that will place him between the passer and the receiver as the football gets there. He is not to bat the ball down but is merely to wave his hands and create a diversion in the eyes of the receiver. The other defender tries to have the receiver hear footsteps, then bumps him as the receiver catches the football. The defenders should not overact by shouting or screaming. The atmosphere should be more game-like.

The Coach

The coach should be confident his team can pass. In the toss-up games the pass will often make the difference. The coach should not "stereotype" his offense by passing only on obvious downs. If a long yardage situation is faced with two downs left, go for half the yardage. Go for the other half with the other down . If an obvious passing down is faced, a quick-count with linemen pass blocking from an up position is effective for pocket protection. Provide adequate time in practice when nothing but the passing game is emphasized.

Chapter 8

Strengthening Types of Multiple Slot-T Pass Protection

The Multiple Slot-T pass protections can be broken down into two techniques as far as the blocking is concerned. They are aggressive and passive. One or both sides of the offensive line can be blocking these techniques depending on the action of the backfield, the time factor, the direction of the quarterback, and the release of the football by the quarterback. The offense includes five types of pass protection: the pocket or cup, the sprint pass, the play action, the moving pocket, and a protection for quickly thrown passes.

The Sprint Pass Protection

Unless the quarterback has outstanding speed the sprint pass is of little use. He has to be a running threat to the defense for the sprint pass to be effective. If the purpose of sprinting out is to gain more time to throw, the moving pocket protection will provide this for the quarterback with average speed. For the sprint pass the weak side linemen will use passive blocking, while the center and the strong side are using aggressive blocking. The defensive alignment will require some blocking adjustments. The linemen on the side of the sprint, by using aggressive blocking, are attempting to prevent the defensive people from penetrating. Their intent is to wall that area until the quarterback has sprinted past. These strong side linemen and the center will fire into the outside half of the defensive linemen and maintain contact as long as they can. If there is no defensive lineman in the area of a lineman who is blocking aggressively, he will fire out to make contact with a linebacker. He will not go more than one yard beyond the line of scrimmage. If no contact is made he will backpeddle quickly, looking to the inside and outside to pick up a block. If there is still no contact he will make an effort to block any color in the area of the quarterback.

A lineman who is blocking passive must have his man over or away from the sprint. If the man is over he will raise quickly from the snap into a crouched position with his fists clenched and even with his chest. He will then butt the defensive lineman while gaining leverage to the side of the sprint. His hands are at chest level so that he can butt an opponent by merely raising his elbows. This butting action will break the charge of the opponent. The inside leverage will prevent the opponent from taking the short route toward the quarterback. If the opponent goes around the block from the outside the passive blocker can give considerable ground while staying between the opponent and the quarterback. If a defensive lineman is aligned to the side of the sprint, a lineman who is blocking passive will have to be aggressive and reach block, maintaining contact as long as possible. Figure 8.1 shows the blocking of the linemen for the sprint pass.

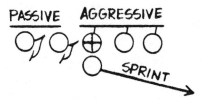

Figure 8.1 Sprint Pass Blocking

For the sprint pass protection the fullback will go after the defensive end on the side of the sprint. He does not wait for the end to apply pressure before attacking him. If the defensive end is into the backfield when the fullback arrives the fullback will body block him. If the end is rushing cautiously from the outside with considerable outside leverage on the quarterback, the fullback will butt the end and allow the quarterback to cut inside or choke down for the pass. If the fullback can hook the end, considerable pressure is now placed on the secondary and the linebackers.

The tailback, without motion, cannot successfully be used to flood the sprint side. He will be used as a trail blocker for the quarterback. Motion of the tailback to the sprint side can be used to flood the sprint side. After the motion, the tailback can streak deep to clear the sprint side for the quarterback or a short receiver. Figure 8.2 shows how the sprint pass protection would apply for a 5-4 defensive alignment.

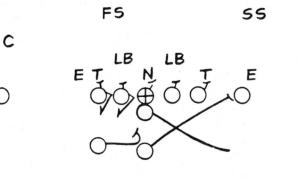

Figure 8.2 Sprint Pass
Protection vs. 5-4 Defense

The general rule for any pass protection blocking is "over" whether it is a lineman or a linebacker. If a linebacker drops quickly the offensive lineman can help in another area. It is important to emphasize to the lineman that his range in a blocking area is much greater than he realizes. Praise should be given to a lineman who has checked his area and gone beyond what would normally be expected of him. The linemen need to be aware of where the quarterback will be setting up for the pass. The type of defensive pressure they feel will help, but it is also significant that the quarterback not scramble unless he has to. Stunting from the defense should not be a problem for the sprint pass. The linemen who are blocking aggressively and have a lineman in an over position should go after that lineman if he slants toward or away from the sprint side. The lineman who does not have a man over him can backpeddle or fold inside or out to pick up a stunting linebacker. If the defense is stunting frequently, the lineman who does not have a man in an over position will deviate from firing the customary one yard. Coaching points and adjustments are necessary when encountering a stunting defense. The short passing game, the sprint pass, and the play action are very effective against a stunting defense.

One year we had a tremendous passing game with the quarterback who was mentioned earlier and the finest group of receivers I have coached. Graduation took practically all of the talented interior linemen. In the ten games we played we faced ten different defenses all designed to contain the quarterback by a cautious outside rush and a stunting defense to the inside. Our running game was virtually nil and it was no secret we relied heavily on the pass. When we played teams that we were physically equal to, because of the highly effective passing game, the game was no contest. However, the teams with the strong linemen would overpower us. If we failed to gain on first down the pressure was on and we weren't able to consistently move the football. If there is any doubt concerning which is more desirable, an outstanding line or an outstanding backfield, I am convinced the people up front make the difference.

The sprint pass protection in the Multiple Slot-T offense is referred to as "10 protection" when the sprint is toward the strong side, and is called "30 protection" when the sprint is to the weak side. The protection is called in the huddle between the formation call and the pass play call. Figure 8.3 shows the sprint pass to the strong side of the 200 formation, and the caption underneath shows how a simple square-out to the flanker would be called. The caption gives the exact words used in the huddle to communicate the pass play.

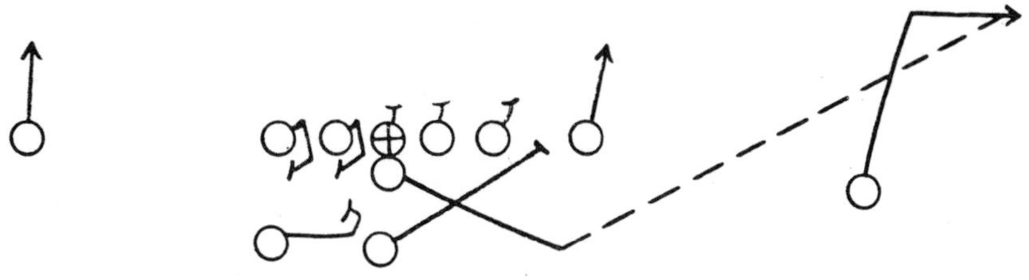

Figure 8.3 "Right Two . . .
Ten . . . Twenty-Eight Pass"

The "Right Two" gives the formation, "Ten" is the protection, and "Twenty-Eight Pass" is the #2 back in the eight zone. The only things not communicated are the routes of the tight end and the split end. The called route is to the #2 back. The ends have a learned route. An influence of practice time for the square-out routes will usually produce a three man pattern. These are discussed in more detail in the next chapter.

For the 30 protection, which is the sprint to the weak side, the center, the weak guard, and the weak tackle block aggressive and the strong side linemen block passive. Most of the time the strong end will remain to block the defensive end on that side. The fullback goes after the defensive end on the weak side, and the tailback forms a wall to the outside with a three-step action to help the fullback with the end if the end comes upfield quickly. The reason for this is because the defensive end can get to the quarterback quicker since his alignment is just outside the weak tackle. For this reason the fullback fires inside quickly to prevent the end from smashing and the tailback protects if the end takes the outside route. Figure 8.4 shows the 30 protection from the 300 formation.

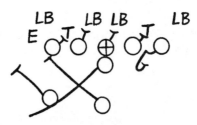

Figure 8.4 Right 3 30 Protection
vs. Split-4 Defense

If an alignment places two defensive people outside the weak tackle they are both in a position to apply immediate pressure on the quarterback. This isn't likely, but the fullback and the tailback can block these two if they do. A "dump" pass or flare control pass to the tailback would be damaging to the defense if both men did smash.

The Play Action Protection

For teams who throw very little (less than ten times) per game or teams who don't mind throwing on first down, the play action pass is a tremendous weapon. This is especially true if the running play, from which the action pass is taken, is a threat. At least one play action pass should be developed from the most effective running play of any offense.

Aggressive blocking is used by all members of the offense for the play action protection. Their assignments are essentially the same as they would be for the running play except, of course, for the receivers. Usually the play action releases only one receiver unless the pass is to a back or the formation has provided two wide receivers. The strong side end, when he is in a tight end alignment, will block the defensive end on his side unless the tight end is the called receiver. If he is the called receiver the pass will be a short one.

The Multiple Slot-T has three play action series. The fullback-over-tackle (which is called R34 and L33), the inside trap toward the formation (which is R42 and L21), and the dive away from the formation (which is R43 and L24) are the three running plays that involve the play action pass. These actions are merely protections, similar to the ten and the thirty protections. Several passes can be thrown from these actions by calling the receiver's number and the zone he will run his route to. For the fullback-over-tackle and the dive protections, the guard to the side of the protection will pull to block the off-side end. For example, for Right 34 protection, the right guard would pull to pick up the off-side or back-side end. In Left 24 protection the right guard would pull to block the off-side end. When the guard pulls, a back who is involved in the play fake fills the space for the pulling guard and blocks any penetration. A linebacker who reads the pulling guard will not be able to key the zone to which the pass is thrown. The trap play action does not involve the on-side guard pulling. The trap running play involves a pulling guard, but it is not necessary to pull this guard for the trap play action pass. The guard blocks aggressively. Figure 8.5 shows a favorite play action of the Multiple Slot-T from the action of the fullback-over-tackle play.

R2 is the Right 200 formation, 34 is the play action

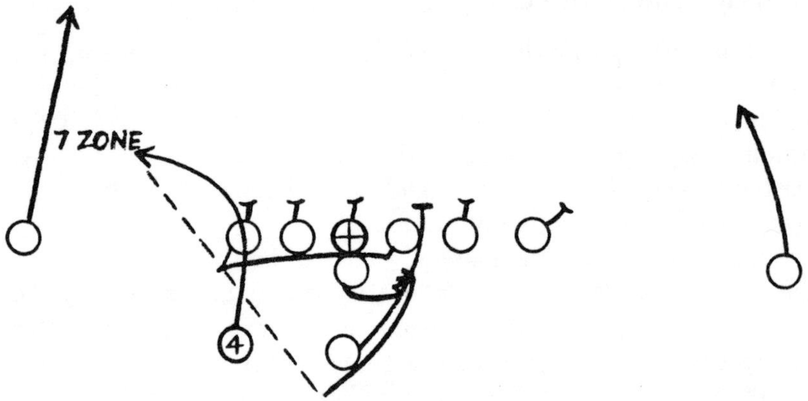

Figure 8.5 R234 47 Pass

protection, and 47 is the #4 back in the seven zone. Other receivers have learned routes which will be discussed later.

Figures 8.6, 8.7, 8.8, and 8.9 show the three play action pass protections from Right and Left formations. Keep in mind the on-side guard always does the pulling for the 34-33 and the 43-24 protections. The center will seal for this guard when there is an even defensive alignment. A pass play is given, in the figures, to complete the scheme of the action pass. These routes will be discussed in the next chapter.

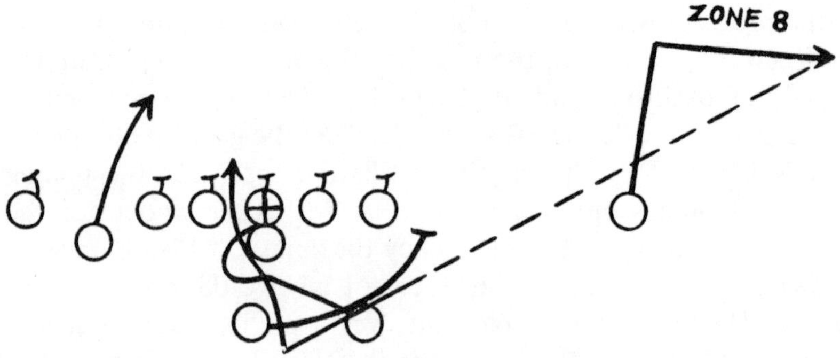

Figure 8.6 L121 Trap 88 Pass

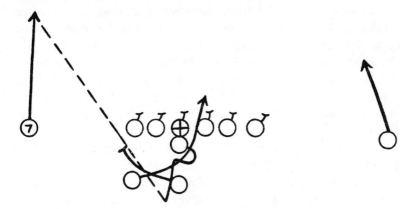

Figure 8.7 R242 Trap 75 Streak Pass

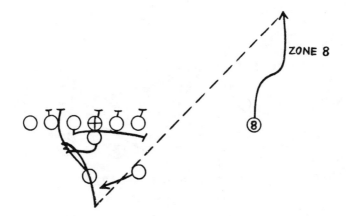

Figure 8.8 L233 88 Take-Off Pass

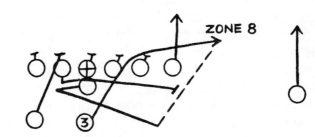

Figure 8.9 R243 38 Pass

Similar to the trap running play, the trap action pass involves the fake to the back with both hands on the football. He will conceal the ball from the defense as much as possible until he sets up to throw, in which case he brings the ball to his chest before executing the delivery. The fullback, who moves behind the tailback on the trap action, blocks the weak side defensive end. The strong side end blocks the defensive end on his side. The slotback can release.

For the dive protection the quarterback will have to sprint toward the strong side. The fake will hold the defensive end on the weak side for an instant, but against most defenses the defensive end will not be blocked. Figure 8.10 shows the 24 dive play action pass to the fullback against a 5-4 with an eagle alignment on the weak side. The defensive end on the weak side will be blocked in this alignment.

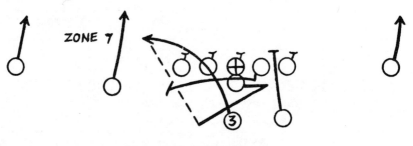

Figure 8.10 L324 37 Pass vs.
5-4 Eagle

The play action passes are good first and second down calls. Usually the play action pass will not be as effective in third and long situations. Some passes are thrown off the action of other plays of the Multiple Slot-T offense but they are not called protections. They fall in a special play category which is ordinarily devised to be successful against a given situation. One of these is the tailback throwing from the power sweep. Another is the fullback throwing from the lead option. Still another is the slotback throwing from the reverse. These will be discussed in the next chapter.

Pocket Protection

For the pocket protection the blockers have four main objectives:

1. Break the initial charge of the defender.

2. Maintain contact as long as possible.

3. Give as little ground as possible.

4. Keep between the defender and the quarterback.

The quarterback is encouraged to stay in the pocket or cup. If the blockers know where he is they can provide maximum protection. The defensive pressure can tell the blocker where leverage is needed.

Generally the linemen will block an area, for the pocket protection, unless the defense is stunting and dealing considerably. Their blocks are passive in that they are not going after the defensive man. However, when the defender gets within striking distance the blocker will meet him squarely. From the snap the linemen will raise quickly into a crouched position with the fists at chest level, similar to a boxer. As the defender gets near enough for the blocker to throw his elbows up and out he will do so, and blast into the defender to break the defender's charge. If the blocker waits for the defender to get to the bulk of his body the blocker is whipped. After the initial contact, the blocker will begin butting the defender by giving as little ground as possible and fighting the pressure of the defender. If the defender goes around, the blocker will pivot his head and shoulders to a point where he can roll the defender to the ground.

If a lineman does not have a defensive man aligned in an over position, he will raise into the crouched position and look for a linebacker. If his area is not challenged he is free to backpeddle slowly to pick up anyone who is putting pressure on the passer. The pocket protection will free three receivers, with a fourth receiver often releasing as a flare control receiver.

The fullback and the tailback or the powerback, depending on the formation, form the sides of the pocket. They will usually block the defensive ends. The tailback will take one step to the outside with his outside foot and form a base that is slightly wider than his shoulders and to a 45 degree angle with the outside. As the defensive end gets within striking distance the tailback will break his initial charge similar to the way a lineman does. The difference is that the back will have to get his weight a little lower and fire up into the defensive end. The defensive end has more velocity, and therefore more momentum. The back will have to strike with as much power as he can. If the tailback overextends by striking too early, this is all the contact he will be able to make. After breaking the charge he will butt the end as long as the end challenges him. If the end goes around, which will usually be the outside route, the tailback will cut him down with a roll block. He should keep his feet moving when butt blocking.

The fullback uses the same blocking techniques as the tailback, but will take more steps to be in position to form the pocket. Usually the fullback takes three steps. The first step is lateral and taken with the outside foot. This is followed by a 45 degree step with the inside foot. Another step is taken with the outside foot. The base is now formed for the block. Each back fights the pressure of the defender and stays between the defender and the quarterback. If an end does not apply pressure the back can look for a linebacker or any defender who is near the passer. This defender will most likely have his hands up; therefore, his charge should be broken by butting him in the stomach. Pocket protection is called "twenty" protection. Figure 8.11 shows the twenty protection with a streak route to the left end. The caption is the way the play is called in the huddle.

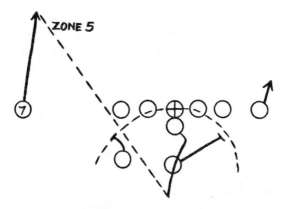

Figure 8.11 "Right Two . . .
Twenty . . . Seventy-Five Streak Pass"

A stunting defense will call for a few adjustments in the blocking for the pocket protection. If the stunts are "X's" and "loops" the linemen will block area. If a defender who is over a lineman slants toward another offensive lineman this lineman would not chase him but pick up a defender, who is probably a linebacker, that is challenging his area. This defender who slants is not an immediate threat to the passer since he has to change his direction again to apply pressure. When protecting against a stacked defense this method is effective. An anchor tackle, such as a split-4 alignment, would normally be assigned to an offensive tackle. However, if the anchor tackle pinched rapidly, the offensive tackle would not chase him but look for the nearest inside linebacker who could be dealing. Stunts and deals can be adjusted to with communication between the line coach and the linemen. As mentioned in an earlier chapter, it is helpful if the offensive linemen are familiar with several defensive alignments they will be facing. When adjustments are necessary, if the linemen can communicate to the coach that they are seeing a particular alignment the adjustments are made easier. If they tell the coach, "a man here and a man there," it is difficult to get a clear picture. The depth and position of the quarterback for the types of pass protection will be discussed in the next chapter.

The Moving Pocket Protection

The moving pocket protection is a variation of the sprint pass protection. The moving pocket merely adjusts for the quarterback who is slower than average. For the moving pocket the linemen to the side of the short sprint block aggressive while the off-side linemen block passive. The fullback goes after the defensive end and the tailback seals behind the quarterback. This type of action is a short pull-up which is effective for throwing deep and to the back side. Figure 8.12 shows the short pull-up of the sprint pass.

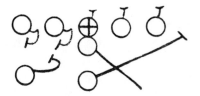

Figure 8.12 The Moving Pocket
Protection

The Quick-Pass Protection

The quick-pass protection involves aggressive action for all blockers. If a tight end is not the called receiver he will block the defensive end. He should blast into the stomach area of the end to keep the end's hands down. The quick protection is used to throw the "quick-outs" to the flankers, to throw to a man in motion who has just turned downfield, and for short "dump" passes over the line of scrimmage.

The action of the quarterback is a two-step motion. If he is right-handed he will drop the left foot back about eighteen inches, then drop the right foot past the left foot to a normal base for the throwing motion. If he is throwing the quick-out to the left he will point the left foot to the target area and fire. When throwing to the right he will swing the left foot across and open to the right as he sets the right foot. He will then fire the ball to the right. The quarterbacks should use the two-step motion each day during the warm-up period.

The Advantages and Disadvantages of Each Type of Protection

The sprint pass protection exerts tremendous pressure on the defensive end, sidebacks, and linebackers. The threat of the run or pass makes it extremely difficult to defense. Considerable running room can be gained by the quarterback since the defense will have to honor any deep receiver. The quarterback is instructed, when he gets to the corner, to throw the football to an open receiver unless a large area of the field opens up. If he is in doubt as to whether he has crossed the line of scrimmage, and a receiver is open, he should throw. The possibility of a penalty is well worth the risk if a touchdown is scored. The sprint pass provides more time to throw than any type of pass protection if the end is conquered.

A disadvantage of the sprint pass is that most quarterbacks will have to "choke down" and set up to throw most of their passes. Some find this as well as throwing on the run a difficult maneuver to develop. The sprint pass cannot be highly effective without a quarterback with above average speed.

The action pass is extremely effective for a limited number of times during a game. Play action completions usually result in long yardage being gained. Either the receiver is behind the secondary or several people, because of the fake, are out of position. A criticism of the play action pass is that if the fake is not effective there is little time to throw the football. Also, the play action should not be effective in a long yardage situation.

The pocket protection provides a blend of adequate passing time and passer-receiver timing. Normally a receiver can run a route and be in a particular area when the quarterback releases the ball. The quarterback retreats deep enough (seven yards) to allow the proper amount of time to throw, even if there is a significant delay of the receivers at the line of scrimmage. Another advantage is that the quarterback is able to throw deep in all directions. A disadvantage of the pocket protection is that the shorter than average quarterback has difficulty seeing. Also, the quarterback usually has to "eat" the football if a receiver is not open, unless he is an excellent scrambler.

The moving pocket protection is excellent for the quarterback who is shorter and slower than average. The fullback will have to be effective with the defensive end. A disadvantage of the moving pocket or short sprint is that, unless the quarterback has a strong arm, he will not be able to throw deep to the off-side.

The two-step quick-pass provides the necessary leverage to release the football across the field. The linemen will be very aggressive to prevent the pass from being batted down at the line of scrimmage. Figures 8.13, 8.14, 8.15, 8.16, 8.17, and 8.18 are a summary of the types of pass protection employed by the Multiple Slot-T.

PASSIVE   AGGRESSIVE   AGGRESSIVE   PASSIVE

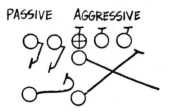

Figure 8.13 Right 10 Protection   **Left 10 Protection**

AGGRESSIVE   AGGRESSIVE

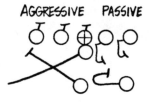

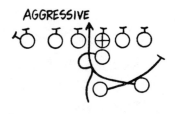

**Figure 8.14 Right 42 Trap
          Protection**   **Left 21 Trap Protection**

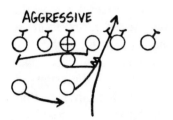

Figure 8.15 Right 34 Protection

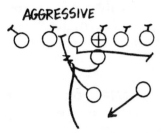

Left Protection

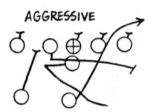

Figure 8.16 Right 43 Protection

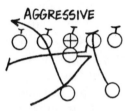

Left 24 Protection

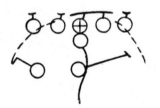

Figure 8.17 Right 20 Protection

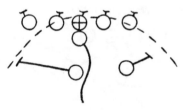

Left 20 Protection

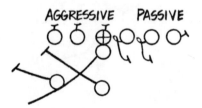

Figure 8.18 Right 30 Protection

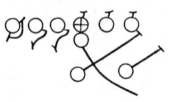

Left 30 Protection

Chapter 9

Organizing Multiple Slot-T Pass Patterns and Routes

The pass that is called in the huddle is identifying the primary receiver and his route. When three receivers are released, which is the case of most passing situations of the Multiple Slot-T, the two secondary receivers run a route that will not conflict with the route of the primary receiver. This is especially true when the called route is a streak or an outside cut. When the route of the called receiver is to the inside the two other receivers run a learned route that is compatible to the called route. Thus, a pattern is set. The purpose of this pattern is to flood or clear a zone for the primary receiver. When the route for the primary receiver is straight or outside, the secondary receivers can run most any route that is in the receiver's repertoire. A few "pet" routes are usually run by these receivers in practice, which actually establishes a pattern even for individual calls.

A strong emphasis must be placed on a receiver, whether a primary or a secondary, running a good route every time. The primary receiver will not need to be reminded as often as the secondary receivers. Considerable self-discipline and pride is necessary for the secondary receiver to run a good route consistently. Sometimes, if the secondary receiver is not putting a lot into his route, the passer will be instructed to throw to him, especially if the receiver is not looking. This will help remind the secondary receiver of his responsibility. When the called route is to the inside, a pattern is set where the secondary receivers must run a definite route. They are not as likely to loaf on the patterned routes. The pass routes for the called receivers will be given first. Some of the companion routes will also be given. A complete diagram of the pattern and the protection will follow.

The Out Routes

There is a simple rule that both ends and backs must remember when their call is an out maneuver. "If you are the widest receiver, run a normal seven yard square-out. If you are not the widest receiver, run a four yard flat route." This is always true if the eight or seven zone is called for a receiver unless a specific variation of the square-out is called for, or if the secondary coverage is not favorable to the regular route. The ends will run the route called for whether they are split or tight. The backs will run the route from a set, flanked, slotted, or motion position.

The square-out for the number eight receiver, the #2 back, and possibly the #4 back, who is in motion to the right, is communicated by calling his number and then the number eight after it. For example, eighty-eight, twenty-eight, and forty-eight for the tailback in motion, is a square-out to the right side. If the receiver is the widest, he will run a normal square-out. If he is aligned inside, he will run the four yard flat route. Figure 9.1 shows how the end will run an 88 Pass from a split and a tight alignment.

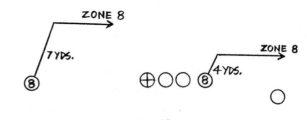

**Figure 9.1 Right 1 Flex 88
and Right 288 Passes**

Figure 9.2 shows how the #2 back will run a 28 route from a flanker and a slot alignment.

Figure 9.3 shows how the #4 back in motion would run the Right 48 pass. When a back is in long motion he will be considered the widest receiver and, therefore, will not have to be concerned with the four yard rule.

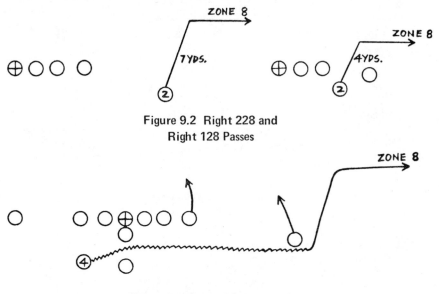

Figure 9.2 Right 228 and
Right 128 Passes

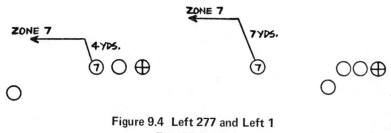

Figure 9.3 Right 2 (40 Strong)
48 Pass

The square-out to the left side is thrown into the seven zone to the number seven receiver, who is the left end, the #4 back who is flanked or slotted, and to the #2 back when he is in long motion. The "four and seven" rule applies to the left side as well as the right side. The square-out is not thrown exclusively to the formation. In fact, most of the time the square-out is thrown to the split end away from the formation, since he is usually the one who has single coverage. Whether the square-out is run toward or away from the formation does not affect the receiver number or the zone number. Figure 9.4 shows the left end, who is the number seven receiver, executing the square-out route.

Figure 9.4 Left 277 and Left 1
Flex 77 Passes

Figure 9.5 shows the square-outs for the #4 back.

Figure 9.6 shows how the #2 back would run a square-out to the left side after long motion.

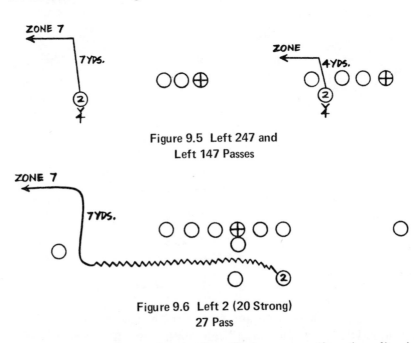

**Figure 9.5 Left 247 and
Left 147 Passes**

**Figure 9.6 Left 2 (20 Strong)
27 Pass**

The type of pass protection that was mentioned earlier is communicated to the blockers just before the pass receiver and the zone is called. The word "pass" is given after the call so that no mistake between a pass or run will be made. If the split end in the Right 100 formation were to be thrown a square-out pass with the pass protection the pocket or cup, the play would be called in the following way: "Right one . . . twenty . . . seventy-seven pass." "Right one" is the formation, "twenty" is the number of the pocket protection, and "seventy-seven pass" is the seven receiver in the seven zone.

More than one route in the seven or eight zone is desirable, therefore some verbal commands are necessary. For example, "eighty-eight quick" or "seventy-seven quick" is a turn-out or quick-out pass to the ends. The word "quick" is inserted after the called receiver. The two-step action by the quarterback is used to throw the quick-out pass. Figure 9.7 shows the quick-out route for the left end from Right 200 formation.

Figure 9.7 Right 277 Quick Pass

The word "quick" communicates to the blockers aggressive blocking. This type of pass protection is not numbered. The quick-out route for the #2 back and the #4 back respectively is Right 228 quick and Left 247 quick. The wide slot (300) formation with the quick-out to the slot is effective, since the safety usually has a bigger cushion than a sideback. (See Figure 9.8)

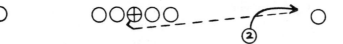

Figure 9.8 Right 328 Quick Pass

Another variation of the square-out is a "deep" call for the inside receiver. The 288 deep, 277 deep, 128 deep, and 147 deep are examples of the deep square-out. The companion route of the wide receiver is a normal square-out. For example, "Right two eighty-eight deep" would call for the flanker to run a regular square-out route. The deep route, for the right end, involves the outside cut at twelve yards from the line of scrimmage. This route is designed to attack the outside zone where the secondary coverage has called for a cornerback or sideback to roll up to take the flanker on the square-out pattern. Figure 9.9 shows how the tight end on a "deep-out" can attack a rotating backfield.

The quarterback will read the cornerback, who is rolling up to take the flanker. He will float the football over the head of the corner to the end. This is an easy read for the quarterback since the cornerback usually has to take the flanker. If the cornerback is loose the quarterback will throw the regular square-out to the flanker. He is reading the "outside-in" coverage as he goes back to set up. The three "out" routes give the passing game an effective outside passing attack.

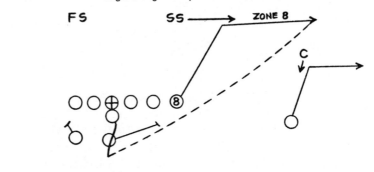

Figure 9.9   (R2)   (20)   (88 deep) vs. Rotating Backfield

The Take-Off Route

The take-off route is thrown in the wide zone, and therefore is called as a seven or an eight zone pass. The command of "take-off" is inserted after the route call. The receiver, who is running the take-off route, cannot run a square-out-and-down route consistently because of the time factor in throwing the football, and also because the receiver loses too much momentum to beat the defender deep. A take-off should normally be run by taking a slight angle to the outside, similar to the square-out. At a point of seven yards a 45 degree turn toward the sidelines is made. On the third step of this turn, the receiver cuts on the outside foot to streak deep. Controlled running at about seven-eighths speed until the final cut would be effective to "velocitize" the defender. Considerable practice by the receiver will be necessary to prevent him from veering to the inside on the streak part of the route. People have the tendency to move in the direction they are looking. An over-the-head catch, after looking over the shoulder to position the ball, will be too advanced for most high school receivers. The tailback in motion may also be able to run a take-off, especially if a linebacker is picking him up. Of course, other receivers will have to clear the eight or seven zones for him. Figure 9.10 shows the take-off route to an end, and Figure 9.11 shows the take-off to a motion back.

When motion, protection, pass play, etc. are communicated, it gets to be a mouthful for the quarterback, but after some familiarity the members of the offense find the calls in the huddle are shortened forms of conversation. If a delay of game penalty

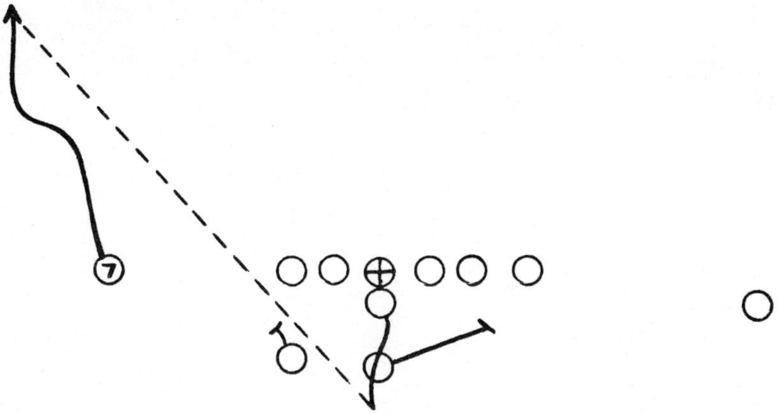

Figure 9.10 R2 20 77
Take-Off Pass

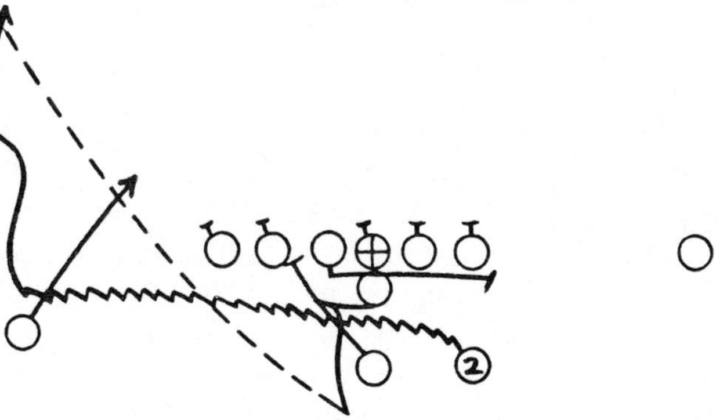

Figure 9.11 L2 20 Strong 33 27 Take-Off Pass

results it is usually caused by the sideline delaying in getting the play to the huddle. Sideline signals and a runner are the methods used to communicate with the quarterback.

The Flag, Streak, and Hook Routes

The flag, streak, and hook routes are run in the five and six zones. For example, "eighty-eight flag" is the right end running a flag route, which is a ten yard and 45 degree angle cut to the outside. He will receive the football looking over the outside shoulder. The flag pass is usually thrown to an inside receiver who is being covered by a safety. Safeties are deep-conscious and are often vulnerable to an outside move. Figure 9.12 shows the 86 flag route from the 200 Formation with the 20 protection.

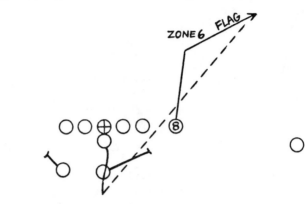

Figure 9.12 R2 20 86 Flag Pass

The 86 flag is similar to the 88 deep square-out route that was mentioned earlier. The flag pass would be a better route against a three deep secondary because the 45 degree angle will hit the safety-sideback seam. The flanker has a learned route for the flag. He will usually run a square-out, but it may be necessary to run him on an underneath post to test the coverage rules of the safety and the sideback. If the sideback covers the flanker, then releases when the quarterback throws the football, he may get back. The crossing action would help neutralize the sideback. Figure 9.13 shows the left end flag with the flanker running a short post route.

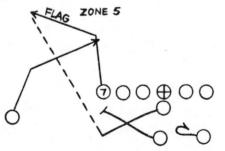

Figure 9.13 L2 (10) 75 Flag Pass

The streak or fly route can be thrown to any of the receivers who are aligned to the outside of the tackles. If a set back runs a streak route it would usually require a play action which would provide a blocker to cover the pass protection blocking for this back. If a receiver has exceptional speed, he will be taught the change-of-pace streak. He merely takes his first few steps at a controlled speed until he has decreased the defender's cushion to about three yards, then turns on the speed. The quarterback will release the football as the receiver gets by the defender. He should not wait for this lead to increase. If the offense has a deep threat from at least one of the receivers an adequate cushion between the receiver and the defender is available to work on. Figures 9.14 and 9.15 show the streak routes for wide receivers.

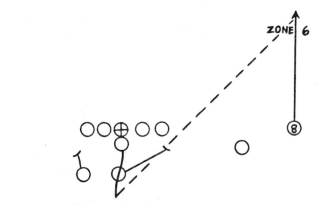

Figure 9.14 R3 20 86 Streak Pass

The receivers who are not called in a route will run a complementary route. Figure 9.16 shows a play action streak to a set back. This is very effective against a three deep secondary.

The hook route is normally run by the ends and the back wider than an offensive tackle. As mentioned earlier, the hook technique involves hooking to the inside. That is, set the inside foot like a square-out and drop the outside foot toward the line of scrimmage, and pivot by turning the shoulders from the outside-in. The receiver will then read the linebackers. The route is referred to as the 6 and the 5 zone hooks. Figure 9.17 shows four hooks from various formations. The secondary receivers run a route to draw the outside coverage.

The hook routes are thrown from any protection other than the quick protection.

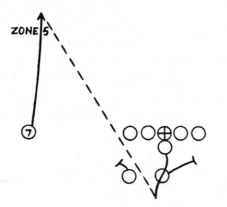

Figure 9.15 R3 20 75 Streak Pass

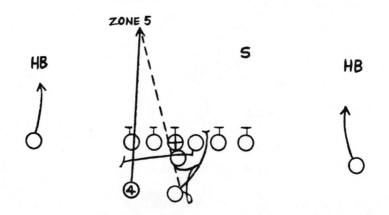

Figure 9.16 R2 (34) 45 streak Pass

The Post and Trail-in Routes

The post is an inside route which usually calls for a learned route by the secondary receivers. They will run a compatible route to the outside to keep the deep post zone clear. The post is thrown to the three and the four zones respectively. If a wide receiver is running a post route, the inside receiver will run almost any route except one that would be in the same deep third of the field. The secondary coverage will often determine the route of an inside receiver. Figure 9.18 shows the 24 post from the 200 formation.

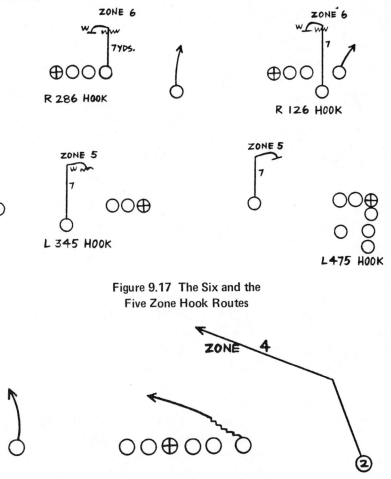

Figure 9.17 The Six and the
Five Zone Hook Routes

Figure 9.18 R 2 24 Post Pass

If the above route were run and the single safety picks up the flanker, a short trail by the tight end might open the seam between the safety and the sideback. The post is thrown from the 20 (pocket), 30 (sprint away), and any play action protection. However, the play action will not usually release the end on the side of the formation as a receiver. The sprint toward the post receiver is not a desirable passing position to throw from.

However, the sprint away from the receiver can get the secondary to move. This will usually cause the inside to open up. Figure 9.19 shows the post against a three-deep secondary. The football should be "laid up" for the receiver, not drilled.

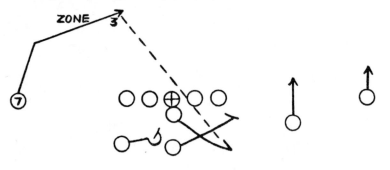

Figure 9.19 R3 10 73 Post Pass

The trail-in route is one of the most effective pass patterns in football. It is a pattern because it involves two receivers, one to test or clear the secondary, and the other to trail-into the vacated zone. Most safeties are deep-conscious while sidebacks are told often about the outside third. A streaking receiver between these two will often cause both of them to keep a sizeable cushion. The outside receiver then slides underneath. The 100 and the 300 formations are the most suitable formations for the trail-in patterns. Figure 9.20 shows the trail-in pattern from the Right 100 formation.

If the word "post" is not called after the receiver and the zone number, the trail-in is the route the receiver will run.

The right end in Figure 9.20 will take a slightly outside path, seven yards deep, then square inside reading the linebackers. If the defensive end in front of him is playing tight, the end will release over the defensive end's face if he needs to. The slotback will streak between the safety and the sideback or corner to test their coverage rules. Figure 9.21 shows the trail-in route from the 300 formation.

If the two defenders are using inside-outside coverage, the trail-in will not be as effective from the 300 formation as it is from the 100 formation. Here the safety will release the streak receiver to the sideback and then be in excellent position to cover the trailing end. However, if the safety drops deep, the underneath

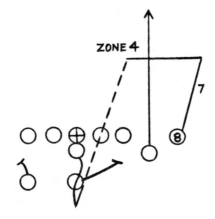

Figure 9.20 R1 20 84 Pass

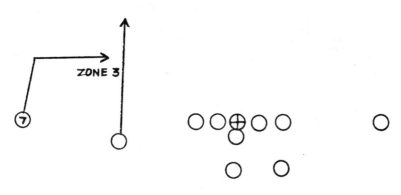

Figure 9.21 L3 73 Pass

zone will be clear. In the 200 formation the flanker can trail. The tight end will "pick" the cornerback, which should open the flanker. Figure 9.22 shows the flanker trail-in from the 200 formation. The end runs the pick route through the near shoulder of the cornerback. The end does not make illegal contact.

The Wide Delay and the Look-In Routes

The number one and two zones are used for the delay and the quick dump passes to the tight receivers, and the look-in routes to the wide receivers. The wide delay route is thrown to a tight end and is highly effective when the linebackers are dropping too far and too quickly to the hook zones. The look-in involves

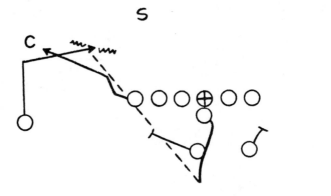

Figure 9.22 L2 43 Pass

the two-step pass protection, while the wide delay can call for any of the types of pass protection except the quick pass protection. The dump pass to the end does use the quick protection.

The wide delay is thrown only to the ends and is called Right 82 wide delay and Left 71 wide delay. The end will block the defensive end near him for two counts. He will then release underneath or between the linebackers, depending on where they are. The most effective formation for the wide delay is the 200 formation. A wide receiver can control the secondary on the side of the delay route. Figure 9.23 shows the side delay from Right formation.

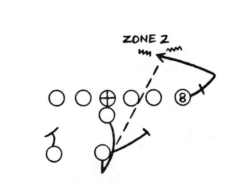

Figure 9.23 R2 20 82
Wide Delay Pass

The wide receivers will streak. The depth of the tight end is controlled by the linebackers. Usually his release to the inside is four yards across the line. Variations of the wide delay are the 82 and the 71 quick passes. These are effective if the linebacker on the side of the tight end is smashing or is playing too close to the line of scrimmage. The two-step protection is used. (See Figure 9.24)

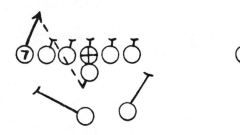

Figure 9.24 L2 71 Quick Pass

The look-in pass is thrown in front of the defender and to the outside of the underneath coverage. The wide receiver will take one step downfield with the outside foot, then drive off this foot at a near 25 degree angle. The quarterback fires the football as soon as he has executed the two steps and gets the football in throwing position. A sizeable cushion by the secondary allows the look-in to be effective. (See Figure 9.25)

The look-in routes are numbered 71 and 41 to the left. To the right they are 82 and 22.

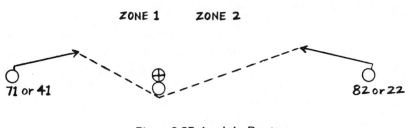

Figure 9.25 Look-In Routes
to Wide Receivers

The Underneath Post Pattern

The underneath post pattern involves three receivers. Two of these receivers will clear a zone for the primary receiver. The weak side end is the primary receiver. This end, who is a split end in most formations, runs a route to the zone farthest from him that has been cleared by two other receivers. Figure 9.26 shows the underneath post patttern from the Right 300 formation. It is called 78 pass to the Right and 87 pass to the left.

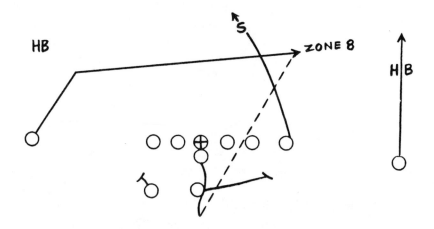

Figure 9.26 R2 20 78 Pass

The flanker streaks and the tight end runs through the near shoulder of the safety. This will clear the deep coverage. The receiver and especially the quarterback will read the underneath coverage to determine the best time to release the football.

The Tailback and the Fullback Pass Routes

The pass routes for the tailback involve a flare, flat, gut, and seam route. In most situations the tailback will be covered by the linebacker, which is an extremely difficult assignment for the linebacker. A play action would be effective to release the tailback, since the linebacker is more conscious of the run. For the #4 back, who is the tailback in Right formation, the routes are numbered 47 flare, 47 flat, 45 seam, and 43 gut. For the #2 back they would be 28 flare, 28 flat, 26 seam, and 24 gut.

The flare route is a flare control from the pocket protection and a throw-back from the sprint, toward the formation, protection. Figure 9.27 shows the throw-back to the tailback from the Right formation.

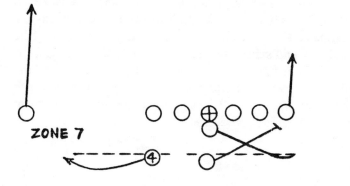

Figure 9.27 R2 10 47 Flare Pass

The split end streaks to clear the seven zone for the tailback. The receivers on the strong side merely run a convincing route. The quarterback will read the linebacker or cornerback coverage.

The Right 47 flat pass is run from the 34 protection and has been a highly successful pass play in the Multiple Slot-T. The tailback should release outside the offensive tackle in order to beat the linebacker. Figure 9.28 shows the Right 47 flat pass. For Left formation the play would be 28 flat pass.

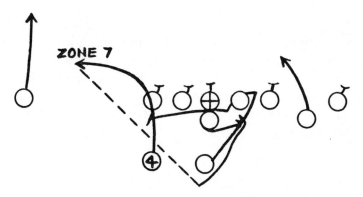

Figure 9.28 R1 34 47 Flat Pass

The split end will clear the deep area. The quarterback makes the 34 fake, then turns his shoulders away from the line of scrimmage and sprints to a set-up position of five yards. Since the pass is short it is not necessary to choke down to a complete stop. He can release the football when his shoulders are turned enough to be on target.

The seam route is used when the weak side linebacker is playing tight and applying considerable pressure on the passing game. The tailback should release inside the defensive end. If he releases across the end's face the end will likely allow a back to release inside of them provided the end is not close enough to the back to hold him up. The ends are more conscious of the pass rush than delaying receivers. Figure 9.29 shows the 26 seam route from Left formation with sprint protection.

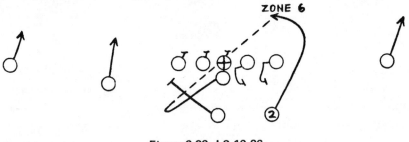

Figure 9.29 L3 10 26
Seam Pass

The quarterback will have to set up from the sprint and turn his shoulders toward the receiver. He should fire the football and throw for the eyes of the receiver. As he sets up he will read the nearest linebacker.

The gut route is very effective against a three deep secondary. The secondary can be spread with the 300 formation. If an adjustment is not made, where a linebacker becomes a safety, the tailback can get open deep. The 34 and 33 protections would be used to give a play fake to hold the linebacker. Figure 9.30 shows the gut pass, which is called Right formation 43 gut and Left Formation 24 gut.

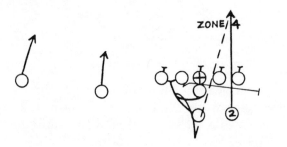

Figure 9.30 L3 33 24 Gut Pass

A good play fake should hold the defensive end on the strong side long enough to throw the football. If the end needs to be blocked, the 200 formation could be used. The quarterback will release the football with his elbow high to keep the pass up so that the receiver can run under it.

The only pass the Multiple Slot-T passing game has to the fullback is a flat route and is an action pass. For Right formation the pass is 38 and for Left formation the pass is 37. The dive play action protection, which is Right 43 and Left 24, is used. The guard on the side of the dive fake will pull to block the defensive end on the strong side. The strong side receivers will streak or run a deep zone route to free the short area for the fullback. After the dive fake the quarterback will sprint toward the strong side. The defensive end on the weak side is not blocked when the weak tackle has an over or outside defensive tackle, but a good dive fake should hold him; also, the quarterback is sprinting away. Figure 9.31 shows the 38 pass from Right 300 formation.

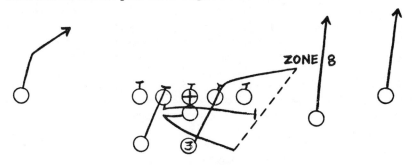

Figure 9.31 R3 43 38 Pass

For all passes that involve the pass protections mentioned in Chapter 8, the pass numbers merely identify the primary receiver and the zone in which he will run a route. The verbal commands after the numbers call for a specific maneuver. Secondary receivers, when they are involved in a pattern, have a learned assignment. When they are not involved they will run a convincing route that will not interfere with the primary receiver.

The Screen Passes

The Multiple Slot-T passing game includes a strong side screen pass to the slotback and a weak side screen to the tailback.

These receivers will release inside the defensive end for the reasons mentioned earlier. When they pass the end they will have to return to the backfield some three yards to be in position to receive the pass. The linemen on the side of the screen and the center will block for two counts, then sprint approximately ten yards to be in the interference area. The strong side screen is run only from the 100 formation.

The quarterback will set up for an instant, at the normal seven-yard point, then recede another five yards. Before he releases the ball the quarterback will read any close color to the receiver. The fullback and the linemen away from the screen will block normal pocket pass protection. Figure 9.32 shows the tailback screen, while Figure 9.33 shows the slotback screen.

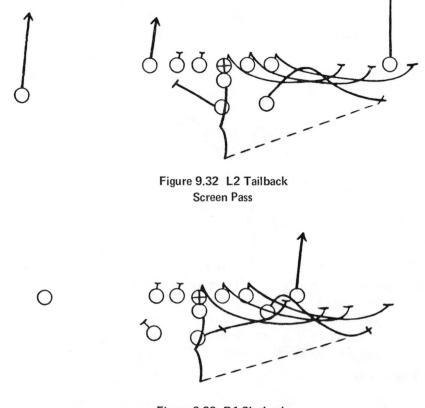

**Figure 9.32 L2 Tailback
Screen Pass**

**Figure 9.33 R1 Slotback
Screen Pass**

A double screen has been effective where one side of the line releases after a one count delay, while the side the screen will be thrown to releases after a two count delay

The Draw

The draw is run from the 20 or pocket protection. The fullback is the ball carrier. The play is called Right and Left 20 draw. If the quarterback is right-handed he will open to his right as he sprints back to set up. He will bring the football to his chest as he would for the pass. The fullback waits for the quarterback to bring the football to him. The quarterback hands the football to the fullback with his right hand. To do this he has to turn his right shoulder in a clockwise motion to prevent shoulder contact with the fullback and be able to execute a smooth hand-off. The linemen will atempt to maintain inside leverage and force the defender outside. The center blocks aggressive and tries to move his man one way or the other. A common mistake of linemen is to think it is all right to let the defensive linemen in—then the back can run by them. Good contact by the offensive linemen is essential for a successful draw play. During the season that was mentioned earlier, in which we relied heavily on the pass, we seldom got back to the line of scrimmage when the draw play was used.

Special Passes

Most offenses contain finesse plays. The Multiple Slot-T contains three finesse passes that are thrown from the action of running plays. Each one of these passes has scored. An easy touchdown that is scored from a finesse or gimmick play has a demoralizing effect on the defense. One of the passes is thrown from the action of the lead option. Another pass is thrown from the slotback reverse. Still another is thrown by the tailback from the action of the power sweep. If the tailback, slotback, or fullback is not capable of throwing the football proper substitution can be made, in most cases, without tipping the play to the defense. The 17 or 18 option pass is thrown by the fullback to either the split end or the tight end who has run a drag pattern across the field. The fullback has also dumped the pass to the tailback who has been released by a linebacker. Figure 9.34 shows the lead option pass from the Right 200 formation.

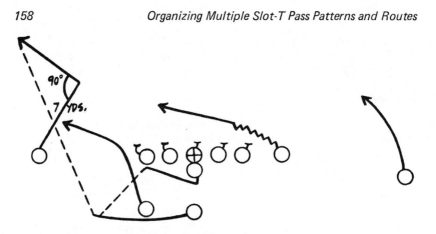

**Figure 9.34 R2 17 Option Pass
to the Split End**

When the option pass is called, the split end, tight end, and tailback run the routes that are shown in Figure 9.35. The primary receiver is identified by "split end," "tight end," or "tailback." The lead option pass is thrown only from the 100 and the 200 formations. The split end, who seals the linebacker on the lead option, runs an "in-out" route.

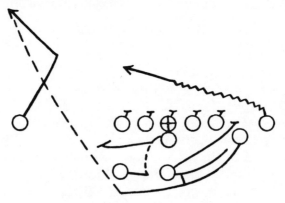

Figure 9.35 R1 27 Reverse Pass

The slotback reverse pass has similar routes for the ends as the lead option pass. This pass is run only from the 100 formation. Figure 9.35 shows the slotback reverse pass, which is identified as Right 127 reverse pass and Left 148 reverse pass. The split end is always the primary receiver unless otherwise indicated. The quarterback blocks the defensive end on the weak side.

The third finesse pass play is the 46 or 25 power pass, as shown in Figure 9.36. Usually this pass is effective when the safety and the cornerback are coming up too quickly. The strong side end will run a deep out route. The tailback is the passer. It is possible to release the slotback in the flat, but this is not normally done unless a coaching point would call for it. The weak side guard does not pull.

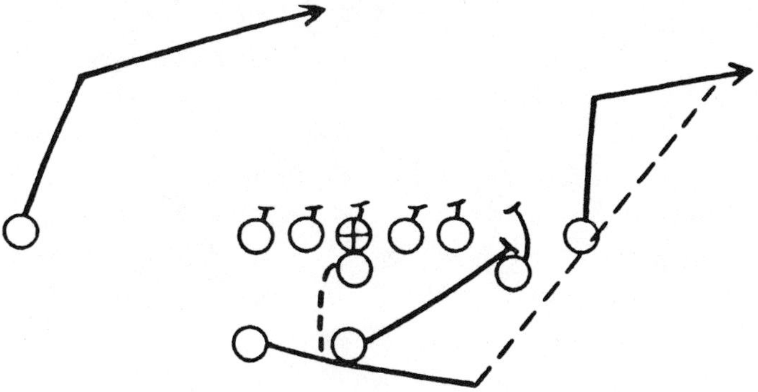

Figure 9.36 R1 46 Power Pass

PART 4

Multiple Slot-T Game Mechanics

10. Preparing the Multiple Slot-T Game Plan

11. Attacking the Defense with the Multiple Slot-T

12. Multiple Slot-T Blocking Charts

Chapter 10

Preparing the Multiple Slot-T Game Plan

The offensive game plan, like the total game plan, is merely a tentative schedule of what you hope to accomplish to defeat your opponent. Only the game itself will determine what you can and cannot do. A coach who begins with a game plan and sticks to it to the bitter end, only to lose by a slim margin, may say after the game, "We had a good game plan; our opponent just out-lucked us a time or two." Perhaps if the coach had broken his plan earlier his team would have scored the few points necessary for victory. I like what Coach Tommy Prothro of U.C.L.A. and the Los Angeles Rams said concerning the game plan. His statement was similar to this: "When you're up to your butt in alligators it doesn't do much good to remember that what you meant to do was drain the swamp." Many coaches spend considerable time preparing a plan, practicing these plans all week, getting the athletes emotionally motivated, then the evening before the game have the attitude, "the game is out of our hands now. We have done everything we can, what will be will be." The biggest test of the coach is still to come. How the coach conducts himself, as far as the battle of wits between himself and his coaches against the opposition's coaches, is the greatest single factor in winning and losing. I have been successful and unsuccessful enough in this mental confrontation to know that it was this battle of wits that either won or lost the close games. It was not the game plan.

In a game where you are heavily favored (two or more

touchdowns) the game may be closer than most people expect, but you will usually win. The same thing is true if you are the underdog by a considerable margin. You may make it close but you will usually lose. When you are neither the favorite nor the underdog by more than two touchdowns, the preparation for the game, the performance of the players, and the conduct of the coaches during the game decides the winner. Statements of "tough luck" and "they are just lucky" often follow the games of narrow defeat. I'm reminded then of the old cliche, "luck favors the prepared mind." Luck is oftentimes an excuse, which when made in front of players, has damaging effects on team morale. Many players and coaches are superstitious to some degree and, if they are convinced they are not lucky, confidence can be destroyed, which could cause them to "choke" in game-turning situations. I personally try to leave the word luck out of any game outcome. I do not want to get into a heavy discussion concerning luck and fate, but I do think it is important not to recognize them as factors that determine victory or defeat.

DISCOVERING OPPONENTS' WEAKNESSES

There are four general areas of the opponent that are considered when preparing the plan to attack their defense:

1. Personnel
2. Alignment weaknesses of their defense
3. Techniques and coverages
4. Their ability to make necessary adjustments

If considerable information concerning these four areas is available the week before the game, a solid game plan can be formed. However, all too often, only the game itself will provide the necessary information. This is why the game plan has to be flexible enough to provide a productive offense.

Defensive Personnel

When evaluating the opponent's personnel it is important to give the opponent the benefit of the doubt concerning overall ability. The individual weakness of a particular position of the opponent's defense should not be discussed with members of the offense. Considerable overconfidence can be developed if they are led to believe a particular position is vulnerable. The coach should plan to attack this area unmercifully if this weakness appears true, but should let the game itself show the offense that a particular area is weak. I have found that over-selling the opponent's personnel is more constructive to provide emotional stimulation for the members of the offense. A challenging attitude is certainly more desirable than expecting an easy time of it. If there is a definite weakness in the personnel of the defense perhaps it would be wise to say very little either way.

Alignment Weaknesses of the Defense

Only the personnel make a defense impenetrable. All defenses have some areas that can be attacked. Coaches often place their best personnel in areas of a particular defensive alignment where known alignment weaknesses occur. All members of a defense certainly have to function as one. A single breakdown often results in a score. The alignment weaknesses of several common defenses and how to attack them will be discussed in Chapter 11.

Defensive Techniques and Coverages

The techniques the linemen, linebackers, and the ends use, as well as the secondary coverages the opponent has been known to use, are important considerations when organizing the plan of attack. If these techniques and coverages prove to be true early in the game, the game plan can then be used to its fullest extent. Often, however, the opponent will change to combat the strengths of your offense. One of the first things I want to know when the game gets under way is how the defense is playing our short slot formation, especially in the immediate area of the slotback and the strong side end. If the off-tackle area is jammed by placing a defensive tackle outside the strong tackle or aligning the defensive end inside the strong end, the six or five hole, depending on Right or Left formation, cannot be run effectively. However, if this alignment is the one employed by the defense, other areas are open. A monster in front of the slotback merely provides a one-on-one situation, which will not discourage us from running into the off-tackle hole.

When coaching the offense to attack the opponent's defense during the preparation week, it is not necessary or effective to show the offense all of the possible adjustments by the opponent. Over-coaching may result in this case. The fundamental alignments of the opponent's defense with some variations they have been known to use will build a sound, confident attitude for the offensive personnel. Of course, the coach is aware of these possible adjustments and has in his plan the alternatives of how to attack them. The techniques that are used by the defensive linemen, the linebackers, and the ends can be attacked for fundamental soundness. For example, if a linebacker closes quickly to defense the dive, a play fake could open a dump pass to an end who curls in behind this linebacker. If a defensive end has an open stance to the outside with the technique of playing the quarterback but also helping with the pitch man after the pitch is made, he is vulnerable to the crack block of the split end when the quick-pitch (Right 47 or Left 28 quick-pitch) is run. These and other techniques and how to attack them will be discussed in the next chapter.

Defensive Adjustments

If the opponent has prepared their defense for the things your offense does best and is able to make the necessary adjustments when you show them something else, it could very well be a long afternoon or evening for the offense. They are forcing you to change your plan while they are able to stick to theirs. Offensive and defensive strategies are more often guessing games. If the defense has adjusted favorably it does discourage the offense from running a particular play. In a situation like this, special plays become a strong influence. It would be unfortunate if a team were defeated by a slim margin and the losing team failed to use a special play they had worked on during the week of preparation.

Some coaches feel it is unsound football to improvise a play during the course of the game. The philosophy that a play has to be run many times before it can be run in a game is sound football, but does not apply completely in modern football. Many teams employ several defenses and even change during the preparation week to adjust to your offense. The only things that restrict the offensive play selection in modern football are the rules of the game. Certainly a high risk is taken when running a play that requires considerable finesse, and more risky is the execution of an improvised play, but it is necessary to take chances when time is running out and you are behind. It is also necessary to take chances when attempting to crack a defense that has adjusted to and defeated every offensive thrust you have attempted. Of course, several factors such as the weather, score, time to play, etc., will determine the amount of risk one should take. An unnecessary risk might backfire and break open a game that was otherwise a stand-off. This would provide the armchair quarterbacks an opportunity to get into the game. The soundness of football is more in the fundamentals of the game and less in the run, pass, and punt philosophy.

The philosophy of the opposing coaches is important when preparing the Multiple Slot-T game plan. Their basic approach to defense is significant when planning the attack. If they believe in bending a little but not breaking, taking the yardage they are willing to give, then having a surprise for them when they begin to tighten up, would be one approach to solving their defense. What the opposition's thinking is when defensing a passing attack will be another important consideration. Most coaches will not drift far from their basic philosophies when preparing a game plan. Those who do will usually put their philosophy to the test. They will realize they have been doing things either the wrong way or the right way. I have been hurt as well as helped when changing the basic defense to encounter an exceptionally powerful offense. It is worthwhile to run a special defense, since you do have something to fall back on if it fails. Generally if the game is a toss-up the opposition will stick to their basic philosophy of defense.

Utilizing the Scouting Report

Many high schools have a difficult time obtaining an adequate scouting report on an opponent. They either do not have a coach available to scout or they are forced to send an inexperienced one who can't possibly get the necessary information by himself. Having an adequate number of coaches, we are able to compile considerable information about our opponent. We send junior varsity coaches or other coaches and friends who are experienced in scouting, exchange films with our opponent, borrow films from teams our opponent has played, talk to coaches our opponent has played, and use last year's film and scouting report. In most situations we are able to predict with reasonable consistency what our opponent will most likely do in different situations. A good scouting report and sound game mechanics are vital weapons.

The Responsibility of Coaches During the Game

It is vital to have the offensive coach, the offensive line coach, the defensive signal caller, and the secondary coach on the sidelines during the game. This may or may not be four different coaches, depending on the individual coaching staffs. In addition to these coaches I also have a coach on the sidelines who moves up and down the field, in the box, and keeps an eye out for significant things the offensive and defensive coaches might miss. He will also talk to players who have come out of the game, but I don't usually expect much knowledge from them. They are on the field carrying out their individual responsibilities and making contact with the opponent. Beyond this they don't know much about what is going on.

A qualified coach in the press box is very valuable. He should be in voice contact with the sidelines, via telephone or such, and will provide the opponent's offensive and defensive alignments to the sidelines. He should be very familiar with the game plan.

The Halftime

The brief delay in the game for the halftime provides little time to get much done, but I believe a lot can be undone during this time. Games have been lost at halftime. I prefer the majority of this time be spent for rest and making the necessary physical adjustments for the second half. About the worst thing that can be done is to shout at each other and hear a stampede of cleats running around. It is necessary that the players avoid excitement during the halftime period. Their mood should not be clouded by a coach who has given them vague adjustments for the second half. We should realize our players are getting tired and cannot grasp considerable sophisticated instruction. The adjustments that are made should be as simple as possible. Generally, the halftime period can be best utilized if the majority of it could be used for rest and quiet. If adjustments are necessary, which is usually the case, the coaches should talk in deliberate tones to prevent interference with other coaches and to provide the best possible communications between coaches and players. I certainly don't want any visitor in the dressing room taking up valuable time.

Coaches, managers, trainers, team physician, etc. are the only people who should be in the dressing room.

Mental Factors

If you are the heavy underdog, a game plan should still be prepared with the idea of winning. Most of the time you won't win if you are more than a two touchdown underdog, but with a good game plan you might make it closer than you realized. This might also enable you to seize an opportunity for an upset if the situation permits. Stranger things have certainly happened. It is difficult to go into a one-sided contest optimistic. Instead of waiting until the game to get up for it and let the emotional factors encourage your athletes, it would be wiser to prepare a sound, realistic game plan in relation to what you think you can and cannot do against your opponent.

On one occasion, our next opponent was far superior to us physically. They had defeated a team, by a sizeable margin, who had defeated the defending state champions in our classification. My plan was to try and make the game as close as we could, but I had an enthusiastic assistant coach who was from the area of this out-of-town opponent and he was returning home and wanted to win the game in the worst possible way. We had exchanged films and I showed the one where our opponent had completely demolished the above-mentioned team. Our players were awed but showed considerable enthusiasm during the week of practice. We worked hard on a plan to stop their crushing ground game and had little time to spend on their passing game, but were willing to gamble since their passing game appeared very weak. The assistant coach spent many hours studying the films for keys. We were prepared mentally (the team and the assistant more than I, for I was facing what appeared to me to be the inevitable) and the night of the game were emotionally high. Our opponent was apparently flat. The combination of these two produced a 6-0 victory for us. This doesn't happen very often, but this victory will remain as one of the most memorable of my coaching career. On other occasions I have experienced defeat from a lack of preparedness when I felt we were too mismatched.

When you are the favored team by a sizeable margin it is important to stick to the basic offense in preparing the game plan.

The mental factors become very apparent when an "it's-in-the-bag" attitude develops. To combat overconfidence, I have found it is best to carry on practice as normal, allow no horseplay or relaxation that is not ordinarily allowed, and keep a formal atmosphere during the pre-game activities in relation to noise around the dressing room, etc. The strangest situation I have faced in coaching is trying to predict when the team is emotionally prepared for a football game. All coaches perhaps try to detect the mental attitude of their players prior to the game, but to no avail. The practice week, the development of a game plan, how well the coaches sell the plan to the players, and the pre-game ceremonies are a few factors that affect the mental attitude of the players going into a contest.

GAME PLAN ORGANIZATION—COACHES' MEETINGS

When organizing the offensive game plan for the next opponent the coaches meetings will include:

1. viewing last year's game film
2. looking over last year's scouting report
3. going over this year's scouting report with the scouts
4. preparing cards that show the defensive alignments, tendencies, stunts, etc.
5. making tentative decisions on areas of our offense we will concentrate
6. adding new plays, if any
7. making a tentative practice schedule of the coming week.

Our squad comes in on Saturday morning following our game on Friday night. This gives us the opportunity to check on the injuries, work off some of the soreness with fifteen or twenty minutes of light calisthenics and running, and to look at the game film of the night before.

On Sunday afternoon or early evening we have a coaches' meeting, at which time we go over the scouting reports, study films, and make the important plans for the coming week. The simple question we ask when preparing the offensive game plan is, "How can we gain enough to beat our opponent?" The rest of our staff meetings are held during the final hour of the school day, in which all of the coaches have a plan period.

Our practice on Monday is usually light as far as contact is concerned. On this day we do most of the teaching in relation to our opponent. We also correct as many mistakes as we can from the previous game. Conditioning is another vital part of Monday's practice. Timewise we are out about an hour and a half. Our junior varsity plays their games on Mondays, which usually begin around 5:00 p.m. This allows our varsity coaches to observe our younger players and helps us keep in touch with the total football program.

Tuesday is our heavy contact day, in which we put our offensive thoughts to the test. If we aren't able to accomplish against our scout team what we have tentative y planned for our opponent, then we are going to evaluate our game plan. If we cannot execute against them we certainly won't be able to against our opponent. Of course, we require that the scout team do, as nearly as possible. what our opponent's defense will be doing and not react to our offense the way they normally would.

Wednesday's practice involves polish and execution. Any contact that we have on this day is for specific purposes, such as pass, punt, or extra point protection. We do close Wednesday's practice, however, with some brief "mean" drills, such as "bull-in-the-ring" or other one-on-one confrontations.

Thursday's practice is light. If weather permits we will wear our game uniform without shoulder or hip pads. We will go through part of our pre-game warm-up, work on kick-off coverage, kick-off returns, punt returns, check offensive and defensive adjustments, etc.

On Fridays we insist that the players come to school on time and do not skip any classes or get off from school without the head coach's permission. At the end of classes they will go home for something to eat and get off their feet for awhile. To insure the players do get rest and will have a time to prepare for the game mentally we want them back at the school at 5:30 if we are playing at home. This gives them time to rest, be taped, etc. This period between 5:30 and when we take the field for warm-ups, which is at 7:15, is a quiet one. There is no more talking than is necessary. We do not want the players seeing or talking to anyone outside of the football family from the time they get to school until after the game. For games in which we play across town, the players usually return at 5:00 p.m. Out-of-town games are handled differently because of the travel time.

Chapter 11

Attacking the Defense with the Multiple Slot-T

The four primary considerations of preparing a game plan, which were mentioned in the previous chapter, are the basic criteria to follow when beginning the attack on the defense. The first method of attack would be on the inferior personnel, if there are any, and the alignment weaknesses. This is usually done with the ground game. If this appears to be a too conservative approach in the first two or three series of downs, testing the techniques and the coverages would be next. Using motion, the pass on the first down, and finesse plays are other methods of attempting to solve the defense. Most coaches would agree on a "four yards and a cloud of dust" philosophy of offense because that is usually the safest way to go. Most teams, however, do not have sufficient personnel to do this.

The first play of the game for our offense is to run an inside play simply to help take the jitters away. A play with a high degree of execution would be very risky on the first play of the game. It is also important to not lose yardage on the first play. This could cause the offense to be off-balance for a few plays and could affect team poise.

After the first play from scrimmage we immediately begin thinking of the play that will provide the first down. Third down situations are certainly difficult to convert, especially if they are more than one yard. An offense that can move the football consistently on the ground and blend in approximately fifteen or so passes with a fifty percent completion ratio, would be an adequate production effort if it provided the two or three touchdowns that are usually required for victory in high school. However, if the offense has the defense completely off-balance with the pass, the passing game can be used more frequently.

On one occasion our plan was to try to establish a respectable running game to prevent our opponent from zeroing in on a pass. We knew we would have to throw the football to win. However, our passer and receivers got hot early in the game and we threw the football two out of three times. We built a three touchdown lead in the first half from which our opponent was not able to recover. We defeated an equal opponent by four touchdowns because we had a good passing game and weren't afraid to use it. The shift, the use of motion, the passing game, and the finesse plays are instruments that are designed to throw the defense off-balance and get the offense rolling.

THE SHIFT

The shift, from one formation to another, is designed to force the defense to make an adjustment before the football is snapped. If they do not adjust properly, weaknesses in their alignments and responsibilities occur. We would then attack these weak areas. The shift is not mandatory on every play, but when it is used it is employed from the 400 (power I) formation.

The quarterback gives the command of "Shift" when the offense has lined up in the Power I formation and paused long enough for the defense to align to it. The quarterback puts his hands under the center, when he commands the shift, to assure the defense is in position. On occasion, the offense can run a play or throw a pass from this formation on the shift command. When the command to shift is given the members of the offense, who are involved in producing one of the other formations, move to their new alignment. Wide receivers will assume the three point stance when they get to this new position. A receiver seven or more yards from an interior lineman moves on the snap from center, not from the quarterback's cadence. He may not hear the quarterback at all times. Figure 11.1 shows how the Left 400 formation becomes the Right 100 formation after the shift. The broken circles represent the new alignment of the backs and the ends after the shift.

Notice that the shift from the Left 400 formation to the Right 100 formation results in moving only two members of the

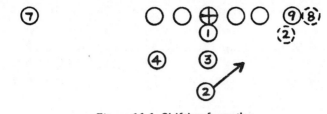

Figure 11.1 Shifting from the
Left 400 Formation to the
Right 100 Formation

offense. The right end flexes another yard and the second man in the I becomes the slotback. This will require the defense to move some people to make the adjustments to this new offensive strength. How many people they move and whether they are linebackers, secondary men, or both will determine the offensive point of attack. Figure 11.2 shows the shift from Right 400 formation to the Right 100 formation.

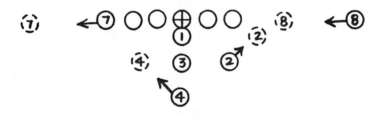

Figure 11.2 Shifiting from the
Right 400 Formation to the
Right 100 Formation

The shift from the Right 400 to the Right 100 involves moving more members of the offense. The right end tightens while the left end splits. The powerback becomes the slotback and the second man in the I becomes the tailback. This is especially true when they found how easy it was to adjust to the shift that is shown on Figure 11.1. Figure 11.3 shows how the shift occurs from Right 400 to the Right 300.

The shift can occur from either the Right or the Left 400 formations to any of the other formations. However, the shift from the Left 400 to the Right 200 involves only one man, the second man in the I, moving to a flanker position. This is not usually done since it requires no significant adjustment by the defense and only wastes time. If the 200 formation is desired, the flanker will either be employed without a shift or will be sent in motion to that side. The shift from the Right 400 to the Right 200 does not affect the defensive adjustments to that side. Figure 11.4 shows that shift.

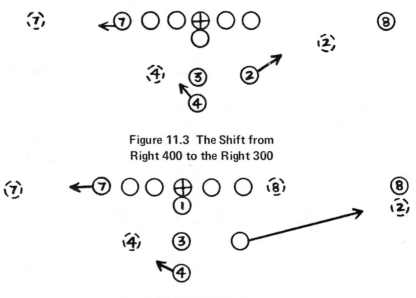

**Figure 11.3 The Shift from
Right 400 to the Right 300**

**Figure 11.4 The Shift from
Right 400 to Right 200**

This shift is of little value if the defense has already honored our right side as the strong side of the formation. After the shift the strength is still to the right. We are also bringing a split end in and replacing him with another wide receiver. A shift of this kind would only result in the cornerbacks or sidebacks loosening for the wide receivers. The members of the offense are instructed not to shift when the 200 formation is used unless otherwise notified. This also helps prevent a delay of the game penalty, since the shift from a set-back to a flanker takes a considerable amount of time. When shifting from the Right 400 formation to the Right 100 and the Right 300 formations it does not change the show of strength, but does move several offensive people to which the defense must adjust. The shift from the Left 400 to the Right 100 and the Right 300 or from the Right 400 to the Left 100 and Left 300 formations moves a minimum number of people but it changes the show or strength. A simple system of "same, opposite, no shift" can be used when specifying from which of the power I formations the shift will occur. "Same" means if a Right formation play is called, the shift will occur from the Right 400 formation. "Opposite" would indicate the shift from the Left 400 formation if a Right formation play were called. Generally the shift will occur from the "opposite" formation since the shift in the show of strength is usually more desirable than moving a few people around but staying in right or left formation. The shift is used from the Right 400 formation to the Left 400 formation. As mentioned earlier, the quarterback will get under the center and bark "Shift," then remove his hands, stand slightly upright, and make sure the people involved in the shift have moved. He will then continue with the signals. He will do this, for a brief moment, even when the shift is not used unless the "two-minute" signals are in effect. To make recognition of the shift simpler for the members of the offense they are instructed to use the "opposite" shift unless the "same" shift or "no" shift is called.

THE USE OF MOTION

Strong side or weak side motion is used to force the defense to make still another adjustment before the snap. When "weak" motion is used by the slotback, the strength of the formation changes. The defense must adjust to this strength. "Strong" motion, by the tailback, adds more strength to the strong side. As mentioned in a previous chapter, "20 strong, 20 weak, 40 strong, and 40 weak" indicate the desired motion. The motion of the back is a significant tool when attacking the defense with the Multiple Slot-T. More motion will be discussed when the attacks on some common types of defenses are discussed.

AUDIBLES

Audibles are used to change the play at the line of scrimmage. The extent to which an offense uses audibles should determine the system that is used. For an offense that checks-off considerably, ten or more times per game, an infallible system should be used that the defense could not detect when repetition occurs. Such a system would involve calling two sets of two-digit numbers. If the first two digits are the numbers of the play called in the huddle, the play is changing and the next set of numbers is the new play. This system works well if all members of the offense are listening to these sets of digits each time the quarterback calls signals. However, if a team seldom checks the play, members of the offense will start ignoring the numbers or become confused when the infrequent check-off is called.

Another system which gets the attention of the members of the offense and is effective when the play is changed only a few times during the game is the use of colors. One color is used to change the play while the other colors are insignificant. For example, if a play that was called in the huddle is changed at the line of scrimmage and the color that indicates a change is blue, "Blue Thirty-four, Thirty-four" would indicate the play had changed to play 34. The new play is called twice to make sure all members of the offense have heard it

Most teams do not find it necessary to check-off many times during the course of the game, but it is worthwhile to have a system of audibles. The Multiple Slot-T has used both systems effectively. The colors are probably best if the members of the offense are not exceptionally alert.

Most of the check-off situations involve an unusual alignment in the hole to which the play has been called. A stacked or loaded alignment in that hole will usually result in the play being changed. The play would simply be changed to a hole nearby that provides normal blocking. The change might also be made to take advantage of an unusually large gap that has been created by the misalignment of the defense. For example, if 42 trap is called, and there are defensive linmen in each gap by the center, the play would probably be changed to the three or the four hole. Most check-offs will result from plays that have been called in the one, two, three, or four holes. When the fake audibles are used the quarterback is instructed to use numbers that will correspond with the backs and these holes. This would mean using twenty-one through twenty-four, thirty-one through thirty-four, and forty-one through forty-four as fake audibles. This will complicate the keying of check-offs by the defense. An exceptionally alert quarterback could call any of the plays of the Multiple Slot-T at the line of scrimmage, but it would take considerable concentration.

STARTING THE BACK IN MOTION

The audibles are also used to start the back who is in motion. The back will start his motion when he hears the color of the audible, provided the play does not change. If the play is changing his motion is canceled. The snap is timed from the color part of the audible so the back will know about how much time he has to be in the proper place at the proper time. Usually his speed is about three-quarters effort.

SIGNAL CALLING

Using the shift, audibles, and motion takes a few more seconds at the line of scrimmage than average. It is important that the quarterback have the play before or very soon after the referee begins timing the play. About 16 to 18 seconds of this time will be spent at the line of scrimmage.

The offense should be at the line of scrimmage with twenty seconds left to get the play under way. After the formation has been set long enough for the defense to align with it, the quarterback will put his hands under the center and command "Shift." As soon as the members of the offense have shifted, but without delay, he will give the "Odd" or "Even" defensive alignment call. This call is for blocking and for the path of the ball carrier. The next command is "Hike," at which time all members of the offense assume their down stance. The quarterback will then give a fake or a live audible, for example, "Blue thirty-three, thirty-three." Next he will slightly drag out a "Set." If the snap is on one the next command is "hike," at which time the center will snap the ball. If the snap count is three, the signal would be "Hike . . . Hike-Hike," which is a non-rhythmic count. The combined signals with a snap count of one are, "Shift . . . Odd defense . . . Hike . . Blue thirty-three, thirty-three . . Set . . Hike." It is possible for the snap to be at four points of the signals. A pre-shift snap at the command of "shift," from the knees at the first "hike," and either on the first or third "hike" after "set." If the quarterback is running short of time when he gets to the line of scrimmage he will call "no shift" and pick up the signals by calling the odd or even defense.

READING THE DEFENSE

An average quarterback in emotional stability and alertness can learn to read the defensive linemen and linebackers in relation to checking-off to another running play. It may be difficult for all but a highly trained quarterback to anticipate the stunts of linebackers. However, if an opponent has provided us with keys, the quarterback can learn to read some of them. We can practice flare and dump passes, or whatever the best approach is during the week of preparation.

The simplest read is for the quarterback to check the hole of the called play. If it looks normal, call fake audibles and then run the play. If it appears difficult, use the live color and change the play to a hole nearby. When employing the option, the quarterback must read the technique of the defensive end in relation to pitching early, normal, or keeping the football.

The most difficult read of the quarterback is certainly the secondary coverage when throwing the football. Even if he reads correctly he has to be in the proper throwing position and release the football on time. Whether the defense is a zone or man, with or without good underneath coverage, three or four deep, rotation or invert, which wide receiver, if any, will be double covered, etc. are usually provided by the scouting report. If not, many of these answers are provided soon after the game starts. Several odd and even defenses will be discussed in relation to attacking them with the running game. The three and four-deep secondaries and the man-to-man coverage will also be discussed.

Attacking the 5-4 Defense

To consistently move the football on the ground involves gaining yardage by running directly at the linebackers, simply because they are playing off the line of scrimmage. When preparing an offensive game plan, as far as the running game is concerned, the openings in the offensive line where the defense has placed linebackers is an area that should draw considerable attention. When attacking the 5-4 defense a dive or fullback wedge into the one or two hole should provide more yardage than running into the three or four holes as far as an inside running

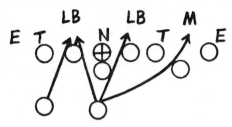

Figure 11.5 Points of Attack
vs. 5-4 Defense

game is concerned. Figure 11.5 shows the general areas a 5-4 Oklahoma defense would be attacked.

The one, two, and the six hole toward the formation are three general areas where the offense would begin attacking a 5-4 defense. The inside and the outside trap plays would also be included in the plan to attack this defense. The outside running game as well as the passing game would be determined by the way the defensive adjustments were made and what the secondary coverage is.

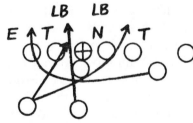

Figure 11.6 Attacking the
Tandem Offset Defense

A variation of the 5-4 front is a tandem-offset or a stacked five defensive alignment. Figure 11.6 shows this defensive alignment and the areas where it should attacked with the inside running game.

The tailback dive can be very effective against the tandem defense. It appears the inside is sealed off but if the center and the guard will execute combination blocks, the back can dive past the linebackers before they can close. To run the four hole, as shown above, will require isolation. The strong guard and the strong tackle have excellent angles. The fullback can isolate the line-backer. The 31 wedge play can also be effective against this defense. The outside trap to the weak side can be highly successful. Figure 11.7 shows the weak side trap by the slotback against the tandem defense. The options, slants, powers, and pitches are good calls against most defenses.

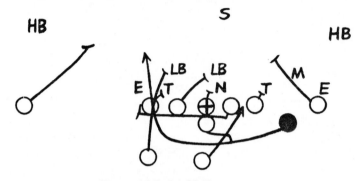

**Figure 11.7 R1 25 Trap vs.
Tandem Offset Defense**

Attacking the 5-3 Defense

The 5-3 defense is effective if the middle linebacker is in the "stud" category. A noseman who is reacting to the first action of the quarterback is hard for the center to block. If the noseman draws the double-team block from a guard, the middle linebacker is virtually free to make the tackle. From the offensive tackles out the defense appears to be an eagle alignment. Standing the noseman up, to be a linebacker, and pinching the defensive tackles down makes the defense a split-four alignment. Figure 11.8 shows the general areas in which the inside running game should attack the 5-3 defense.

The one and two holes should be attacked considerably with the dives, fullback wedges, and the inside traps until the offense is thoroughly convinced those areas cannot be penetrated. The slants and the off-tackle powers should be effective. If the tackles close their alignment from the inside eye of the offensive tackles, the off-tackle area will be open more. The defense will have to stunt and deal considerably if the 5-3 defense is used as their basic defense unless superior personnel is available.

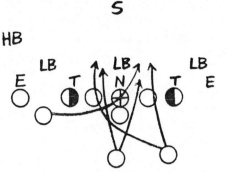

Figure 11.8 Attacking the 5-3
Defense with the Inside
Running Game

Attacking the Split-Four Defense

The best method of attacking the split-four alignment, with the exception of having sufficient speed to run sweep plays, is running at the linebackers. The traps, isolations, slants, and the fullback over tackle should be effective against this defense. The dive to the inside will test the ability of the anchor tackles and the linebackers to close the middle. The short slot formation causes the split-four some alignment problems. If the tackles do not pinch, the inside will be vulnerable. If they do pinch, the off-tackle, especially in the area of the slotback, will open. Figure 11.9 shows the areas in which the Multiple Slot-T would attack the split-four defense.

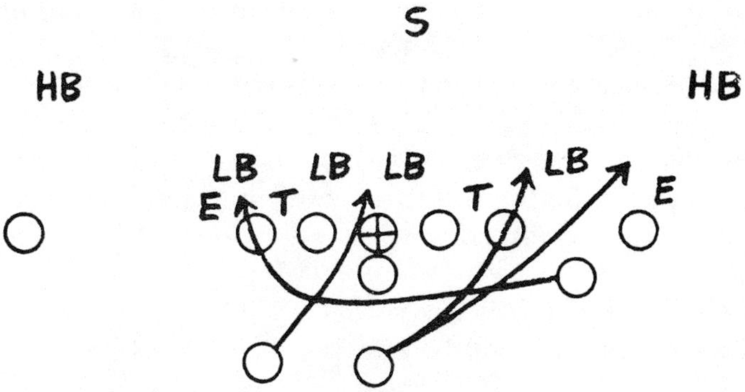

Figure 11.9 Attacking the
Split-Four Defense

The only inside running play that is probably not effective against this defense would be the straight dive into the three or four holes. Of course, the design of the split-four is to be a dealing defense. This is where the guessing game between the offense and the defense begins.

When attacking any defense with the inside running game, the Multiple Slot-T will not usually attack the hole where a defensive lineman is. When a defense has linebackers stacked behind linemen, the Multiple Slot-T would use the isolation and dive plays considerably. If a defense is stunting, the delayed plays are used. The cross-bucks (23X and 44X), the fullback over tackle (33 and 34), the outside traps (25 and 46), and the fullback counter (30 counter) are some of these delayed plays. The techniques of the defensive ends determine the pitch or keep of the option. The alignment of the defensive tackles determines what plays are used to attack the off-tackle area.

Passing Against a Three Deep Zone Secondary

The called routes, especially to the outside, flood routes, and crossing routes are effective against the three-deep zone coverage. If the defense has good underneath coverage by the linebackers, the draw, delay passes, and play fakes will need to be used to keep them near the line of scrimmage.

When the standard square-out route is called to a wide receiver, the quarterback knows the sideback on defense has to cover it. The quarterback simply reads this defender and releases the football if the defender has kept an adequate cushion. The square-out should not be intercepted unless the defender guesses correctly in stepping up and inside. This is risky for the three-deep since the safety is not free to back the sideback up. Patterned passes that release three receivers are the most common passes thrown against the three-deep zone. Figure 11.10 shows a few pass patterns that are effective when attacking the three-deep zone secondary.

Throwing deep, if the secondary is defending the short to medium passes well, will be effective since there is no free safety. The 47 and the 28 flat passes will usually go for considerable yardage against the three-deep secondary if a linebacker can be beaten to the flat. (See Figure 11.11)

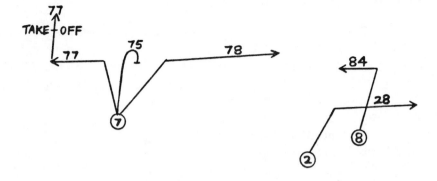

**Figure 11.10 Attacking the
Three-Deep Zone Secondary**

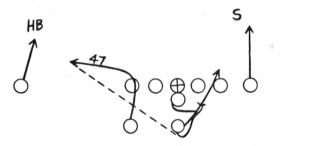

**Figure 11.11 R2 34 47 Pass
Against a Three-Deep Secondary**

Figure 11.12 shows the 84 post pass in hitting the seam between the safety and the sideback.

Probably the best method of attacking the three-deep zone would be to spread it. The 300 formation will spread the secondary and provide considerable room to work on an area.

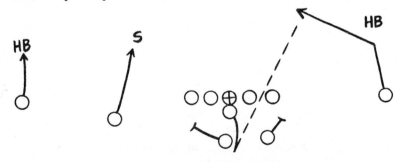

Figure 11.12 L3 20 84 Post Pass

Attacking a Four-Deep Zone

When attacking a four-deep zone secondary, reading the coverage becomes the principle task. There are three common coverages of a four-deep secondary. The "four across the board" coverage involves rotation in the secondary to the strong side of the formation. This is determined by the alignment of the offense or the sprint action of the quarterback. The corner takes the short zone to the side of the strength. The strong safety defends the deep third behind this cornerback. The free safety defends the deep third and the other corner takes the off-third. Another coverage is where either safety inverts while the other three backs take deep third. The "two and two" coverage involves the corners taking the short zones and the safeties defending deep. This is effective in jamming receivers and throwing off the receiver-quarterback timing.

We generally know the different types of coverage our opponent will use. Of course we don't know when they will use a particular coverage, but if we can hurt them in one coverage they probably will not use it for a while. The coverage rules of the secondary should be tested early in the game. It is, however, unlikely that you would want to throw deep, especially in the middle third of the field, since the secondary has a free safety. The "out" routes, the "flags," the "hooks," and the "trail-ins" are effective against a four-deep secondary when they are rotating. Fig. 11.13 shows the 88 flag route against a four-deep zone.

The quarterback reads the coverage from the outside-in. If the cornerback is playing the flanker, he will throw to the flag

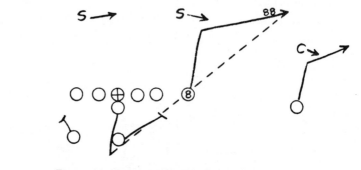

Figure 11.13 R2 20 88 Flag Pass
vs. Four-Deep Secondary

receiver. If the corner is hanging and giving ground the quarter-back will throw to the flanker, who would have to be covered by an inverting safety.

The Right 128 and the Left 147 passes are effective against an inverted secondary. (See Figure 11.14)

Flooding zones is an effective method of defeating a zone defense. Putting three receivers into two zones places tremendous

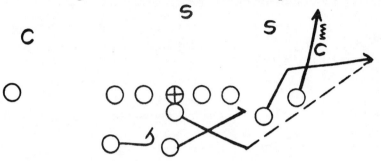

**Figure 11.14 R1 10 28 Pass vs.
Inverted Secondary**

pressure on the defense. Two of these receivers can streak and clear the zone for the third receiver. The slotback or the tailback in motion will help flood a zone even if the secondary goes into full rotation. Figure 11.15 shows a pass pattern that is used to flood a zone.

If the cornerback picks up the man-in-motion, the right end would most likely be open on the deep square out. The man-in-motion streaks and the flanker runs through the strong safety. If a linebacker is used to cover the man-in-motion, clearing

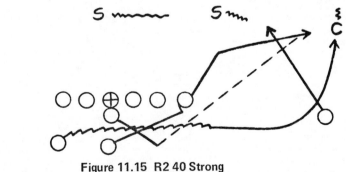

**Figure 11.15 R2 40 Strong
10 88 Deep Pass**

the deep third with the flanker and the right end would make the motion man open on a streak pass. We could also use the 100 Formation and run the 36 or 35 slant with a full set of blockers if a linebacker takes the tailback in motion. If your opponent uses the same coverage you do, attack the areas that you know to be weak.

Defeating a Man-to-Man Coverage

If your opponent uses a man-to-man coverage, be grateful unless he is blessed with superior personnel. Man-to-man coverage requires quality athletes. Picking on the weak man would be one way to attack the man coverage. Throwing the short passes is another method, since the defenders must keep a respectable cushion to prevent being beaten deep. A valuable asset when the offense is facing a man-to-man secondary is that the offensive backs will be covered by linebackers. It would take an exceptional linebacker who could cover a halfback and also play the run effectively. Figure 11.16 shows a pass that would be very effective against a man-to-man coverage. A special play of tackle eligible would be effective against a man secondary.

Being familiar with the types of pass defense your opponent uses is necessary when attacking with the pass. The ability of the quarterback to read the coverage is also a contributing factor. However, the ability of the passer is the most significant factor

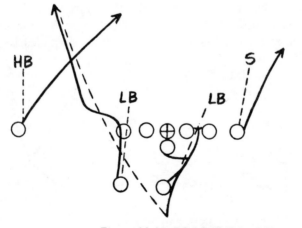

Figure 11.16 R2 34 47 Take-Off
Pass vs. Man Coverage

when attacking with the pass. His ability to be accurate and release the football on time, when the receiver has gotten to a certain place, will make reading the coverage considerably easier. The talanted passer will be able to hit receivers between zones or in the seams of a secondary if he has adequate time to throw.

THE TWO-MINUTE OFFENSE

The most significant difference between the Two-Minute Offense and the regular offense is the signals. The shift and usually the audibles are dispensed with. Quite often the snap count will use the first "Hike" or quick-count for two reasons:

When pass blocking for the pocket protection, blocking from "the knees" (the hands or the forearms on the knees just prior to the crouched position) is very effective. It allows the offensive linemen to see the smashing linebackers without having to snap up into position. Also, at a time when we cannot afford a penalty, it prevents an overanxious lineman from raising into a blocking position before the football is snapped. When the offense gets to the line of scrimmage the quarterback gives the defensive alignment of "odd" or "even," simply to let the rest of the members of the offense know they should get settled because the snap count is soon to follow. In a second or two the quarterback barks "Hike," at which time the football is snapped.

The real test of the coach as a master of strategy is during the final two minutes of the ball game with his team needing a score to win. Blending the play selections with the time-outs remaining and moving the football down the field is well worth the price of admission. I have seen defenses off-balance in the closing seconds of a game because of the offense had a well-poised two-minute attack.

The "out" routes, floods, delays, trails, flares, seams, and flats are a few routes that are effective against a defense with a victory cushion. Using the boundary is important in stopping the clock. We instruct the officals before the game that anyone on the field can call time-out. We instruct the players that they will be told by a coach when to call time-out. The quarterback and the defensive captain are instructed in several situations where they will call a time-out without waiting for the signal from the sidelines.

Chapter 12

Multiple Slot-T Blocking Charts

The method the coach uses to organize and teach the rule blocking is very important. The players should be furnished with a play sheet that is actually a page from the coach's play book. These plays and the individual's assignments should be on one page so that it will appear brief and concise. An explanation of the terminology that appears on the play sheet should be made when the sheets are passed out. The players can either fill out the rules for the holes or the sheets can be furnished with them.

The linemen are blocking by the holes instead of Right or Left formation, therefore the hole and whether the play is a trap, wedge, isolation, dive, etc. is communicated to them. Periodic testing of the rules would be important to assure the coach that the linemen still know them. A page that contains several defenses, and more significantly, the defenses your next opponent will use, could be furnished. The members of the offense could then supply their individual assignments. These work sheets should be checked and even graded by the coach.

On the individual's play sheet, space could be provided for coaching points. These sheets are used frequently during skull sessions, especially during the weeks of pre-season practice. The coaching points and the adjustments of the rules certainly must be made on the Monday prior to the game. Using the rules of the Multiple Slot-T will require few blocking adjustments.

The receivers are furnished a play sheet of the passing game. Their called routes and the passes that are patterned, which involve a learned route for them, are also provided. The backs are provided with a play sheet for blocking and faking as well as for when they are the ball carrier. The following pages contain the individual blocking assignments for all members of the offense and the assignments for the backs when they are not the ball carrier.

For the lineman, the hole and the type of running play is all he needs to follow when carrying out his assignments, but the number of the ball carrier is provided so that he will get the overall picture of the offense. For example, the two hole "trap" communicates a specific assignment. The two hole "wedge" involves straight ahead blocking and firing out quickly. The two hole "isolation" communicates that a back will be helping, so stay with the rule block. A lineman should not be concerned if the hole appears stacked. A "dive" indicates no fold blocking. All other plays that are not specified with blocking instructions after them are base rule blocks. The pass protection assignments are also given on the individual's play sheet. Rule blocking is simple to teach after the players understand the terminology that is used.

POSITION LEFT END

PLAY	ASSIGNMENT
17 OPTION	SEAL NEAREST LINEBACKER
47 QUICK-PITCH	CRACK THE END
27 REVERSE, 17 BOOTLEG	PUSH HB DEEP
25 POWER	INSIDE, OVER, LB, CORNER
25 TRAP	NEAR HB
35 SLANT	OVER, OUTSIDE
43 DIVE, 33, 23X, 23 ISOLATION	INSIDE, OVER, OUTSIDE, NEAR HB
41 DIVE, 31 WEDGE, 21 ISOLATION	RUNNING LANE
21 TRAP	RUNNING LANE
30 COUNTER	RUNNING LANE
42 TRAP	RUNNING LANE
42 ISOLATION, 32 WEDGE, 22 DIVE	RUNNING LANE
44 ISOLATION, 44X, 34, 24 DIVE	RUNNING LANE
36 SLANT	RUNNING LANE
46 TRAP	RUNNING LANE
46 POWER	RUNNING LANE
48 REVERSE, 18 BOOTLEG	RUNNING LANE
28 QUICK-PITCH	RUNNING LANE
18 OPTION	RUNNING LANE
PASSES	
10 PROTECTION	RECEIVER
20 PROTECTION	RECEIVER
30 PROTECTION	RECEIVER
34 AND 33 PROTECTIONS	34- RECEIVER 33- BLOCK AND
43 AND 24 PROTECTIONS	RECEIVER
42 TRAP AND 21 TRAP PROTECTIONS	42-RECEIVER 21-OVER, OUTSIDE

Figure 12.1

POSITION LEFT TACKLE

PLAY	ASSIGNMENT
17 OPTION	GAP, OVER, LB
47 QUICK-PITCH	OVER, LB
27 REVERSE, 17 BOOTLEG	GAP, OVER, LB
25 POWER	GAP, OVER, LB
25 TRAP	GAP, LB
35 SLANT	GAP, OVER, LB
43 DIVE, 33, 23X, 23 ISOLATION	GAP, OVER, LB
41 DIVE, 31 WEDGE, 21 ISOLATION	OVER, LB, OUTSIDE
21 TRAP	LB OVER OR INSIDE
30 COUNTER	RIGHT- GAP, OVER, LB LEFT- LB OVER OR INSIDE
42 TRAP	OVER, INSIDE, LB
42 ISOLATION, 32 WEDGE, 22 DIVE	GAP, OVER, LB
44 ISOLATION, 44X, 34, 24 DIVE	GAP, OVER, LB
36 SLANT	CUT-OFF, RUNNING LANE
46 TRAP	GAP, OVER, LB, RUNNING LANE
46 POWER	CUT-OFF, RUNNING LANE
48 REVERSE, 18 BOOTLEG	GAP, OVER, LB, RUNNING LANE
18 OPTION	CUT-OFF, RUNNING LANE
PASSES	
10 PROTECTION	RIGHT- PASSIVE LEFT- AGGRESSIVE
20 PROTECTION	BASE RULE, PASSIVE
30 PROTECTION	RIGHT- AGGRESSIVE BASE RULE, LEFT- PASSIVE
34 AND 33 PROTECTIONS	BASE RULE, AGGRESSIVE
43 AND 24 PROTECTIONS	BASE RULE, AGGRESSIVE
42 TRAP AND 21 TRAP PROTECTIONS	BASE RULE, AGGRESSIVE

Figure 12.2

POSITION LEFT GUARD

PLAY	ASSIGNMENT
17 OPTION	GAP, OVER, OUTSIDE, LB
47 QUICK-PITCH	GAP, OVER, LB
27 REVERSE, 17 BOOTLEG	GAP, OVER, LB, FOLD
25 POWER	GAP, OVER, LB
25 TRAP	GAP, OVER, LB, OUTSIDE
35 SLANT	GAP, OVER, LB
43 DIVE, 33, 23X, 23 ISOLATION	GAP, OVER, LB, FOLD (ON DIVE NO FOLD)
41 DIVE, 31 WEDGE, 21 ISOLATION	OVER, LB
21 TRAP	ODD- DT WITH CENTER EVEN-OUTSIDE
30 COUNTER	RIGHT-PULL, TRAP 1 ST. TO SHOW LEFT- SAME AS 21 TRAP
42 TRAP	PULL, TRAP 1 ST. TO SHOW
42 ISOLATION, 32 WEDGE, 22 DIVE	GAP, OVER, LB
44 ISOLATION, 44X, 34, 24 DIVE	GAP, OVER, LB
36 SLANT	CUT-OFF, RUNNING LANE
46 TRAP	PULL, TRAP 1 ST. TO SHOW
46 POWER	PULL, LEAD IN HOLE
48 REVERSE, 18 BOOTLEG	CUT-OFF, RUNNING LANE
28 QUICK-PITCH	CUT-OFF, RUNNING LANE
18 OPTION	CUT-OFF, RUNNING LANE
PASSES	
10 PROTECTION	BASE RULE RIGHT-PASSIVE LEFT - AGGRESSIVE
20 PROTECTION	BASE RULE PASSIVE
30 PROTECTION	BASE RULE RIGHT- AGGRESSIVE LEFT- PASSIVE
34 AND 33 PROTECTIONS	33- PULL, BLOCK OFF-SIDE AND 34- BASE RULE AGGRESSIVE
43 AND 24 PROTECTIONS	43- PULL, BLOCK OFF-SIDE END 24- BASE RULE AGGRESSIVE
42 TRAP AND 21 TRAP PROTECTIONS	BASE RULE AGGRESSIVE (NO PULL)

Figure 12.3

POSITION CENTER

PLAY	ASSIGNMENT
17 OPTION	OVER, GAP, LB AWAY
47 QUICK-PITCH	OVER, GAP, LB AWAY
27 REVERSE, 17 BOOTLEG	OVER, GAP, LB AWAY
25 POWER	OVER, SEAL RIGHT
25 TRAP	OVER, SEAL RIGHT
35 SLANT	OVER, GAP, LB AWAY
43 DIVE, 33, 23X, 23 ISOLATION	OVER, GAP, LB AWAY
41 DIVE, 31 WEDGE, 21 ISOLATION	OVER, GAP, LB AWAY
21 TRAP	OVER, SEAL RIGHT
30 COUNTER	OVER, RIGHT-SEAL LEFT / LEFT-SEAL RIGHT
42 TRAP	OVER, SEAL LEFT
42 ISOLATION, 32 WEDGE, 22 DIVE	OVER, GAP, LB AWAY
44 ISOLATION, 44X, 34, 24 DIVE	OVER, GAP, LB AWAY
36 SLANT	OVER, GAP, LB AWAY
46 TRAP	OVER, SEAL LEFT
46 POWER	OVER, SEAL LEFT
48 REVERSE, 18 BOOTLEG	OVER, GAP, LB AWAY
28 QUICK-PITCH	OVER, RUNNING LANE
18 OPTION	OVER, RUNNING LANE
PASSES	
10 PROTECTION	BASE RULE, AGGRESSIVE
20 PROTECTION	BASE RULE, PASSIVE
30 PROTECTION	BASE RULE, AGGRESSIVE
34 AND 33 PROTECTIONS	BASE RULE, AGGRESSIVE
43 AND 24 PROTECTIONS	BASE RULE, AGGRESSIVE
42 TRAP AND 21 TRAP PROTECTIONS	BASE RULE, AGGRESSIVE

Figure 12.4

POSITION RIGHT GUARD

PLAY	ASSIGNMENT
17 OPTION	GAP, OVER, LB
47 QUICK-PITCH	CUT-OFF, RUNNING LANE
27 REVERSE, 17 BOOTLEG	OVER, LB, RUNNING LANE
25 POWER	PULL, TRAP 1ST· TO SHOW
25 TRAP	PULL, LEAD IN HOLE
35 SLANT	OVER, RUNNING LANE
43 DIVE, 33, 23X, 23 ISOLATION	GAP, OVER, LB
41 DIVE, 31 WEDGE, 21 ISOLATION	GAP, OVER, LB
21 TRAP	PULL, 1ST· TO SHOW
30 COUNTER	LEFT- PULL, 1ST· TO SHOW RIGHT-SAME AS 42 TRAP
42 TRAP	EVEN-OUTSIDE ODD- DT WITH CENTER
42 ISOLATION, 32 WEDGE, 22 DIVE	GAP, OVER, LB
44 ISOLATION, 44X, 34, 24 DIVE	GAP, OVER, LB, FOLD
36 SLANT	GAP, OVER, LB
46 TRAP	GAP, OVER, LB
46 POWER	GAP, OVER, LB
48 REVERSE, 18 BOOTLEG	GAP, OVER, LB, FOLD
28 QUICK-PITCH	OVER, LB, FOLD
18 OPTION	GAP, OVER, LB
PASSES	
10 PROTECTION	RIGHT-AGGRESSIVE BASE RULE, LEFT- PASSIVE
20 PROTECTION	BASE RULE, PASSIVE
30 PROTECTION	RIGHT- PASSIVE BASE RULE, LEFT- AGGRESSIVE
34 AND 33 PROTECTIONS	34-PULL, BLOCK OFF-SIDE END 33-BASE RULE, AGGRESSIVE
43 AND 24 PROTECTIONS	24-PULL, BLOCK OFF-SIDE END 43-BASE RULE, AGGRESSIVE
42 TRAP AND 21 TRAP PROTECTIONS	BASE RULE, AGGRESSIVE (NO PULL)

Figure 12.5

POSITION RIGHT TACKLE

PLAY	ASSIGNMENT
17 OPTION	CUT-OFF, RUNNING LANE
47 QUICK-PITCH	CUT-OFF, RUNNING LANE
27 REVERSE, 17 BOOTLEG	GAP, OVER, LB, RUNNING LANE
25 POWER	CUT-OFF, RUNNING LANE
25 TRAP	GAP, OVER, LB, RUNNING LANE
35 SLANT	CUT-OFF, RUNNING LANE
43 DIVE, 33, 23X, 23 ISOLATION	GAP, OVER, LB
41 DIVE, 31 WEDGE, 21 ISOLATION	GAP, OVER, LB
21 TRAP	OVER, INSIDE, LB
30 COUNTER	LEFT-GAP, OVER, LB RIGHT-LB OVER OR INSIDE
42 TRAP	LB OVER OR INSIDE
42 ISOLATION, 32 WEDGE, 22 DIVE	OVER, LB, OUTSIDE
44 ISOLATION, 44X, 34, 24 DIVE	GAP, OVER, LB
36 SLANT	GAP, OVER, LB
46 TRAP	GAP, LB
46 POWER	GAP, OVER, LB
48 REVERSE, 18 BOOTLEG	GAP, OVER, LB
28 QUICK-PITCH	OVER, LB
18 OPTION	GAP, OVER, LB
PASSES	
10 PROTECTION	BASE RULE, RIGHT- AGGRESSIVE LEFT- PASSIVE
20 PROTECTION	BASE RULE, PASSIVE
30 PROTECTION	BASE RULE, LEFT-AGGRESSIVE RIGHT-PASSIVE
34 AND 33 PROTECTIONS	BASE RULE, AGGRESSIVE
43 AND 24 PROTECTIONS	BASE RULE, AGGRESSIVE
42 TRAP AND 21 TRAP PROTECTIONS	BASE RULE, AGGRESSIVE

Figure 12.6

POSITION RIGHT END

PLAY	ASSIGNMENT
17 OPTION	RUNNING LANE
47 QUICK-PITCH	RUNNING LANE
27 REVERSE, 17 BOOTLEG	RUNNING LANE
25 POWER	RUNNING LANE
25 TRAP	RUNNING LANE
35 SLANT	RUNNING LANE
43 DIVE, 33, 23X, 23 ISOLATION	RUNNING LANE
41 DIVE, 31 WEDGE, 21 ISOLATION	RUNNING LANE
21 TRAP	RUNNING LANE
30 COUNTER	RUNNING LANE
42 TRAP	RUNNING LANE
42 ISOLATION, 32 WEDGE, 22 DIVE	RUNNING LANE
44 ISOLATION, 44X, 34, 24 DIVE	INSIDE, OVER, OUTSIDE, NEAR HB
36 SLANT	OVER, OUTSIDE, LB
46 TRAP	NEAR HB
46 POWER	INSIDE, OVER, LB, CORNER
48 REVERSE, 18 BOOTLEG	PUSH HB DEEP
28 QUICK-PITCH	CRACK THE END
18 OPTION	SEAL NEAREST LB
PASSES	
10 PROTECTION	RECEIVER
20 PROTECTION	RECEIVER
30 PROTECTION	RECEIVER
34 AND 33 PROTECTIONS	34- OVER, OUTSIDE 33- RECEIVER
43 AND 24 PROTECTIONS	RECEIVER
42 TRAP AND 21 TRAP PROTECTIONS	42- OVER, OUTSIDE 21- RECEIVER

Figure 12.7

POSITION #2 BACK

PLAY	ASSIGNMENT
17 OPTION	RUNNING LANE
47 QUICK-PITCH	RUNNING LANE
27 REVERSE, 17 BOOTLEG	27- BALL CARRIER 17- RUNNING LANE
25 POWER	BALL CARRIER
25 TRAP	BALL CARRIER
35 SLANT	MOVE LEFT
43 DIVE, 33, 23X, 23 ISOLATION	43-RUNNING LANE 33-MOVE LEFT 23X 23I- BALL CARRIER
41 DIVE, 31 WEDGE, 21 ISOLATION	41, 31- RUNNING LANE 21-BALL CARRIER
21 TRAP	BALL CARRIER
30 COUNTER	LEFT-FAKE DIVE RIGHT-RUNNING LANE
42 TRAP	OVER, NEAR HB
42 ISOLATION, 32 WEDGE, 22 DIVE	22-BALL CARRIER 42, 32- RUNNING LANE
44 ISOLATION, 44X, 34, 24 DIVE	34-OVER, NEAR HB (RIGHT) END (LEFT) 24-BALL CARRIER 44I, 44X- OVER, HB
36 SLANT	OVER, NEAR HB
46 TRAP	IF DT IS INSIDE OT, BLOCK LB IF DEF. T IS OVER OT, BLOCK END
46 POWER	INSIDE, OVER
48 REVERSE, 18 BOOTLEG	48R-BALL HANDLER 24-18- FAKE DIVE 34-18-HOOK END
28 QUICK-PITCH	BALL CARRIER
18 OPTION	BLOCK 1ST. MAN IN SECONDARY
PASSES	
10 PROTECTION	LEFT-BLOCK RIGHT- RECEIVER
20 PROTECTION	LEFT-BLOCK RIGHT-RECEIVER
30 PROTECTION	LEFT-BLOCK RIGHT-RECEIVER
34 AND 33 PROTECTIONS	34-RECEIVER 33-MOVE LEFT
43 AND 24 PROTECTIONS	43-RECEIVER 24-FAKE DIVE
42 TRAP AND 21 TRAP PROTECTIONS	42-RECEIVER 21-FAKE TRAP

Figure 12.8

POSITION #4 BACK

PLAY	ASSIGNMENT
17 OPTION	BLOCK 1ST· MAN IN SECONDARY
47 QUICK-PITCH	BALL CARRIER
27 REVERSE, 17 BOOTLEG	43-17- FAKE DIVE 27R- BALL HANDLER 33-17-HOOK END
25 POWER	INSIDE, OVER
25 TRAP	IF DEF. T IS OVER OT- BLOCK END IF DEF. T IS INSIDE OT - BLOCK LB
35 SLANT	OVER, NEAR HB
43 DIVE, 33, 23X, 23 ISOLATION	33 RIGHT-NEAR END, LEFT-OVER, HB 43-BALL CARRIER 23X, 23 I-OVER, HB
41 DIVE, 31 WEDGE, 21 ISOLATION	21 I-OVER, HB 31 LEFT-HELP OT 41-BALL CARRIER 31 RIGHT-FAKE 44X
21 TRAP	OVER, NEAR HB
30 COUNTER	LEFT-RUNNING LANE RIGHT-FAKE DIVE
42 TRAP	BALL CARRIER
42 ISOLATION, 32 WEDGE, 22 DIVE	32 AND 22-RUNNING LANE 42I-BALL CARRIER
44 ISOLATION, 44X, 34, 24 DIVE	24-RUNNING LANE 44I, 44 X-BALL CARRIER 34-MOVE RIGHT
36 SLANT	MOVE RIGHT
46 TRAP	BALL CARRIER
46 POWER	BALL CARRIER
48 REVERSE, 18 BOOTLEG	18-RUNNING LANE 48-BALL CARRIER
28 QUICK-PITCH	RUNNING LANE
18 OPTION	RUNNING LANE
PASSES	
10 PROTECTION	RIGHT-BLOCK LEFT-RECEIVER
20 PROTECTION	RIGHT-BLOCK LEFT-RECEIVER
30 PROTECTION	RIGHT-BLOCK LEFT-RECEIVER
34 AND 33 PROTECTIONS	33-MOVE LEFT 34-RECEIVER
43 AND 24 PROTECTIONS	43-FAKE DIVE 24-RECEIVER
42 TRAP AND 21 TRAP PROTECTIONS	42-FAKE TRAP 21-RECEIVER

Figure 12.9

POSITION FULLBACK

PLAY	ASSIGNMENT
17 OPTION	OPTIONAL BALL CARRIER
47 QUICK-PITCH	LEAD
27 REVERSE, 17 BOOTLEG	33-17- FAKE 33 43-17- HOOK END 27-BLOCK RIGHT END
25 POWER	BLOCK LEFT END
25 TRAP	FAKE 34
35 SLANT	BALL CARRIER
43 DIVE, 33, 23X, 23 ISOLATION	23X-FAKE 32 231- LEAD 43-MOVE LEFT 33-BALL CARRIER
41 DIVE, 31 WEDGE, 21 ISOLATION	21 I- LEAD 41-MOVE LEFT 31-BALL CARRIER
21 TRAP	MOVE RIGHT
30 COUNTER	BALL CARRIER
42 TRAP	MOVE LEFT
42 ISOLATION, 32 WEDGE, 22 DIVE	44X-FAKE 31 24-MOVE RIGHT 44I-LEAD 34-BALL CARRIER
36 SLANT	BALL CARRIER
46 TRAP	FAKE 33
46 POWER	BLOCK RIGHT END
48 REVERSE, 18 BOOTLEG	24-18-HOOK END 34-18-FAKE 34 48R-BLOCK LEFT END
28 QUICK-PITCH	LEAD
18 OPTION	OPTIONAL BALL CARRIER
PASSES	
10 PROTECTION	RIGHT-BLOCK RIGHT LEFT-BLOCK LEFT
20 PROTECTION	RIGHT-BLOCK RIGHT LEFT-BLOCK LEFT
30 PROTECTION	RIGHT-BLOCK LEFT LEFT-BLOCK RIGHT
34 AND 33 PROTECTIONS	34-FAKE 34 33-FAKE 33
43 AND 24 PROTECTIONS	43-RIGHT FLAT 24- LEFT FLAT
42 TRAP AND 21 TRAP PROTECTIONS	42-BLOCK LEFT END 21-BLOCK RIGHT END

Figure 12.10

Index